Super Foods for
AWESOME MEMRY

Shipra Khanna's first love is cooking, and after winning the MasterChef India Season 2, she has never looked back. Today she is a restaurateur, television food anchor, author, social worker and has her own digital channel. She also conducts demonstrations of how to cook multiple global cuisines.

Super Foods for
AWESOME MEMORY

Shipra Khanna

Published by
Rupa Publications India Pvt. Ltd 2018
7/16, Ansari Road, Daryaganj
New Delhi 110002

Sales centres:
Allahabad Bengaluru Chennai
Hyderabad Jaipur Kathmandu
Kolkata Mumbai

Copyright © Shipra Khanna, 2018

Image copyright © Alamy and Shutterstock
Book illustrations: Prabhjyot Majithia

The information contained in this book is not intended as a substitute for medical consultation with a physician and may not be construed as medical advice or instruction. Instead, readers should consult appropriate health professionals on any matter relating to their health and well-being. Before starting any diet/exercise, you should speak to your physician. All information contained in this book but not limited to text, graphics, images, information, third party information and/ or advice, food, recipes, exercise, diets and psychology are for informational and educational purposes only. No action or inaction should be taken based solely on the contents of this information. This book is not meant to be used, nor should it be used, to diagnose or treat any medical condition. The publisher and the author are in no way liable or responsible with respect to any loss or incidental or consequential damages caused to any person or entity, or alleged to have been caused, directly or indirectly, by use of the information contained in this book.

ISBN: 978-81-291-4950-3

First impression 2018

10 9 8 7 6 5 4 3 2 1

The moral right of the author has been asserted.

Printed by Excel Printers Pvt. Ltd., New Delhi

This book is sold subject to the condition that it shall not, by way
of trade or otherwise, be lent, resold, hired out, or otherwise circulated,
without the publisher's prior consent, in any form of binding
or cover other than that in which it is published.

To my two beautiful kids,
Yadavi and Himannk,
who have been an inspiration at all times.

CONTENTS

From the Chef's Table — ix

Introduction — 1
Salmon — 4
  This Fish Helps to Meditate
Poultry — 13
  A Chicken a Day Keeps Ageing Away
Extra Virgin Olive Oil — 23
  Remember This Oil, Forget Alzheimer's
Avocado — 31
  Untangle Your Brain
Beetroot — 39
  More Power to the Brain
Coconut Oil — 47
  Fighting Bad Bacteria, Fighting Memory Loss
Blueberry — 58
  Berry! To Beat the Blue
Bone Broth — 67
  A Healthy Belly, a Healthier Mind
Broccoli — 76
  The 'Cool' Vegetable

Celery	85
Minding the Migraine	
Green Leafy Vegetables	93
Red Lighting Mental Deterioration	
Walnuts	101
Going 'Nuts'? Have Walnuts	
Rosemary	111
'Nerves' of Steel	
Almonds	119
Fasten Your Seat Belts, Brain on Full Throttle	
Egg Yolk	130
Eggs are Forever	
Dark Chocolate	139
Liking the Heart, Loving the Brain	
The Conclusion	149
Table of Measures	151

FROM THE CHEF'S TABLE
'The way you feel is the way you look!'

Everything is mind over matter, and to keep your mind in a good condition, it is very important to follow a good diet. Here's an effort from my end to make you feel good or at least show you the way one can. I have compiled all the ingredients in this book which help in sharpening the mind, provided one has them in moderate amounts. Having said that, these ingredients will benefit completely only if one's daily routine is balanced with food, exercise, meditation and a healthy lifestyle.

I have made the recipes very simple and easy to follow so that they can be conveniently included in one's daily diet. Food is an important part of our lives and we should be careful with what we consume, and at what time we consume it. A routine is really important to get the desired results.

Every body type is different and hence not every type of food goes well with everyone's system. So, one should omit such ingredients from the diet or recipes.

INTRODUCTION

No brain, no gain! Life is driven by the brain, as the body follows what the brain says. It includes both the conscious and the subconscious mind. Our mind rests while we sleep, but that is only the conscious part of it which is at rest. The subconscious part works in strange ways. The discussions and debates on this have been endless.

Memory has always been an important facet of human civilization. However, it is only in the current phase of human history that it has acquired centre stage. Memory plays a significant role in an environment where we are dependent on technology and gadgets more than ever, while our lifestyle is laden with stress like never before. We can only ignore memory at the peril of forgetting our own self.

I do remember someone saying, 'This is good for the brain,' while we had brain curry on our table. There are many such myths; liver recipes being good for the liver is another one. I have humbly tried to break a vicious circle of jejune conversations around this topic by simply coming up with recipes that will make one healthy, wealthy and wise, and the ingredients used will make for real mealtime conversation in one's day-to-day life.

The way you feel is the way you look. Have you ever come across anyone sleep-deprived looking their best? The answer is but obvious! Good sleep is dependent on the subconscious mind and the digestive system that are working while you sleep. It is important to keep the body healthy so that the mind can command its slave—the body—without any constraints.

Both body and mind work as a guru-shishya team—the slave-master team. The logistics are pretty much the same as one is redundant without the other. Nonetheless, the master is the brain!

The brain consists of the mind, the intellect and every matter that the five senses feel. Food is the only art form that conquers all five senses; so it is evident that the right kind of food can treat everything—from lifestyle, health, addiction to patterns of imbalance, and, like a see-saw, balances one's life to make it better.

Well-being is highlighted in our lives by eating the right kind of food. A variety of dishes makes life more interesting and kills the monotony and boredom that comes with following a specific routine and consuming specific foods.

Having said this, I am in no way undermining the importance of other aspects, like environment and circumstances, which are equally important and without the support of which the mind cannot function in the correct manner.

It has been correctly said that 'too many cooks spoil the broth', as everything works only in the correct proportions. Cherishing the amazing nature-given gifts in abundance is only possible when one understands the holistic methods of life. Ways to use these natural ingredients in the correct manner comprise the soul of the book. The recipes for a good life come from here. At the same time, good sleep, exercise, meditation, etc. are also equally important and one should never ignore these, since combined with the right ingredients, they make a foolproof method to sharpen the mind.

So come with me on an interesting and delicious journey of recipes and ingredients that will make your mind and memory awesome.

SALMON

This Fish Helps To Meditate

Salmon is full of omega-3 fatty acids which help your brain to run smoothly. Feeding salmon to kids can help prevent ADHD (Attention Deficit Hyperactivity Disorder) by improving their focus. These fatty acids can also prevent cancer and kill tumours. Salmon is available in many forms, like smoked salmon which is delicious and can be used in both salads and sandwiches. Consumption of this, along with exercise, good sleep and meditation, can help in increasing concentration.

Saltwater fish as well as legumes, such as kidney beans, are amongst those ingredients that are good for memory and brain development. Salmon is one of my favourite fish; it is very popular and widely consumed all across the globe. Smoked salmon sandwiches are something that I can eat at any hour!

SALMON

Salmon is a freshwater fish which moves to salt water and then migrates back to fresh water. Trout, char and white fish also belong to the same family. People who are health-conscious should opt for it. One of my favourite recipes of salmon is with caper and butter sauce. I remember chef Alex in Jabal Akhdar preparing a delectable salmon dish for me that I can never forget—enjoying the salmon in the middle of the rocky mountains where one could never expect to get something so fresh and so heavenly was a surreal experience. Fish is an amazing ingredient and in addition to being healthy, it can also be flavoured in varied ways. Adding something acidic to the fish is the number-one rule, as it enhances its taste. People who don't like the smell of fish can marinate it in carom seeds for 10–15 minutes, then wash off the marinade and cook it in the flavours they like. Grill it, fry it, sauté it, or barbeque it, fish will always taste good. Another thing about fish is that the river fish will always have a distinct taste from that of the sea fish.

Fish takes 3–4 minutes to cook on each side, depending on its size—whether fillet or whole. Another memorable experience was in Xocho in Getaria, Spain, where we (the chefs and I) got fresh fish from the sea, rubbed salt on it and cooked it over open flame in a mesh, which was especially designed for the fish, occasionally drizzling vinaigrette over it. It took us approximately 20 minutes to cook and it was served with fried garlic and paprika sauce. Yummy! I still remember its taste. Healthy, tasty and simple to prepare—that's what fish is!

Garlic is another ingredient that goes very well with

fish. In fact, I would say fish, garlic and lemon juice form the perfect combination in Western cuisine, whereas if you are preparing fish in Indian style, then the curries and masalas are what you depend on. The Amritsari fish, one of the most popular fish dishes in India, is such an example; it is marinated in spices, chilli powder and lemon juice and then fried.

If we go down south of India, we'll find a huge variety of curries. They make fish in coconut milk and different spices, and the flavours are very distinct from each other. Fried, Chettinad and Andhra flavours are also very popular in India and a must experience, especially for people who love fish. Rawas, an Indian fish, is popularly known as Indian salmon and found in many coastal belts of India.

Oriental flavours also work very interestingly with fish. I love fish with pepper, lemongrass, ginger, garlic, soy sauce, black bean sauce—flavours and combinations are numerous.

It is advised not to eat fish during its breeding season. But nowadays, caviar (fish eggs) is really popular amongst people who crave for exotic food, and is found in a lot of varieties depending on how much you want to spend on it!

BAKED SALMON WITH CAPER BUTTER SAUCE

INGREDIENTS

300 g salmon fillets
2 tsp lemon juice
3 tbsp olive oil
1½ tsp salt
1½ tsp ground black pepper
100 g butter
1 tbsp capers
150 g cream
4-5 slices of lemon
1 bunch kale, washed and chopped

METHOD

Heat butter.

Add salt, ½ tsp pepper, lemon juice, cream and capers. Cook while stirring continuously till it boils, then keep aside.

Toss kale leaves with salt, ½ tsp pepper and olive oil and place on the base of the baking dish.

Cut the salmon fillet in half. Toss with lemon zest, salt and pepper. Place a fillet in the dish on top of the kale leaves, skin-side down. Top with butter caper sauce and a lemon slice.

Bake in an oven at 200°C for 25 minutes.

GRILLED SALMON

INGREDIENTS

200 g salmon fillets
Salt and black pepper to taste
1 tbsp horseradish
2 tbsp olive oil
½ tsp red wine vinegar
Lemon wedges for garnish

METHOD

Heat grill (or broiler) just before you are ready to cook.

In a bowl, combine salt, pepper, horseradish and vinegar. Mix well.

Grease the grilling pan and cook the salmon for 5-6 minutes. Keep brushing with the prepared mix until fish is tender.

Serve with lemon wedges.

CREAMY SALMON WITH DILL

INGREDIENTS

200 g salmon fillets
½ cup cream
2 tbsp fresh dill, chopped
1 tsp grainy mustard
1 clove garlic, finely minced
A pinch of salt

METHOD

Preheat oven to 200°C and line a baking tray with parchment paper.

Place salmon fillets, skin-side down, on the paper.

Mix cream, dill, mustard, garlic and salt.

Spread mixture evenly over salmon and bake for 8-10 minutes, or until flaky.

Serve hot with a squeeze of fresh lemon.

CRISPY COCONUT SALMON

INGREDIENTS

¼ cup desiccated coconut
1 tbsp grated parmesan cheese
1 tsp breadcrumbs
Salt and pepper to taste
1 egg, beaten
250 g salmon, skinned and sliced into 4 pieces

METHOD

Preheat oven to 180°C.

Mix the shredded coconut, breadcrumbs, cheese and salt together in a bowl. Set aside.

Dip the salmon in the egg and coat both sides with the coconut mixture.

Bake the salmon for 15-20 minutes, flipping once, until the salmon is cooked and the coconut crust is slightly browned and crisp. Serve warm.

FISH CAKES

INGREDIENTS

1 egg
250 g salmon fillets, boiled and mashed (look out for the tiny bones, if any)
2 tbsp olive oil
1 large sweet potato, boiled and mashed
1 tbsp parsley, finely chopped
2 tbsp onion, finely chopped
1 tbsp lemon juice
½ tbsp chilli sauce
½ tbsp salt
1 ¼ tsp paprika
½ tsp black pepper

METHOD

Preheat oven to 180°C.

In a large mixing bowl, combine all the ingredients except oil. Mix until well-combined.

Line a baking pan with parchment paper.

Make small balls of the mix, flatten them and place on the parchment paper at 1" distance from each other.

Brush each cake with oil and bake for 20-25 minutes on the middle rack until light golden in colour.

Serve with a spicy sauce of your choice!

Food for Thought:
There are some ingredients that go very well with fish. My favourite ingredients with fish are garlic, lemon juice, paprika and olive oil. Whether you bake it, or grill it, or steam it, these flavours are always savoured with fish.

If you are a fish lover and love eating healthy too, it's the best choice but having said that, always remember, depending on whether the fish is from the sea or the river, it will have a different taste, and that's why some have a strong smell and some have no fishy odour at all. So now you know why something smells fishy!

POULTRY

A Chicken a Day Keeps Ageing Away

One of the most widely consumed bird in poultry is chicken! There is definitely a reason why it is so. Diets rich in choline protect your brain from the effects of ageing. The nutrients from the B vitamin family is found in foods like chicken and eggs and their consumption may help in improving memory and brain development. Of course, at the same time, we cannot deny the important role of good sleep and exercise in enhancing memory.

Poultry is another recommendation for those who want to lose weight or eat healthy as it is a high protein diet. Though chicken has no taste of its own, it is still very popular. You can cook it whole, stuffed or in curry and it will take in the flavours and cook until tender. Whether cooked in Indian or any other Asian flavours, chicken always tastes good. In Asia, it is quite popular, especially in India as we have a lot of vegetarians and chicken does not have any specific smell that can averse them. Chicken can be cooked with its skin intact, and my favourite recipes with skin are the baked ones where, when the skin is baked, it becomes crisp and the fat melts, adding flavour to the dish and the sauce.

There are two types of chicken that are available in the market—broiler and desi, as we call them. As the names suggest, broiler is farm-bred, whereas desi is wild. And being wild, it has more food value and tastes really different. But, at the same time, being wild, it is a difficult nut to crack and takes longer to cook. Our modern life suffers under the tyranny of time and as such, its demand is very low, especially in metro cities where people don't have the leisure to cook. The wild chicken cooks best in curries while broiler is good for any type of cuisine.

Chicken soup is recommended during fever or cold as it has healing properties and is also a comfort food. One of my comfort recipes is chicken soup with lots of veggies and noodles, and I can have it anytime of the year. Another very popular recipe in India, whether in the north or the south, is fried chicken or batter fried chicken which can be mixed with a sauce later and savoured. Recipes which come to mind when one has to cook chicken are numerous—tandoori, grilled, fried, steamed or curry. I prepared tandoori recipes with chicken after I inaugurated tandoor at Le Cordon Bleu, Paris, and taught the international students how to use it to cook delicious recipes. This book has a lot of recipes which one can savour and are easy to make and serve as well!

What came before—the chicken or the egg? This question has been asked for centuries, and history has proved that this theory is inconsequential if both are cooked right, presented correctly and relished!

CHICKEN PICCATA

INGREDIENTS

2 boneless chicken breasts, sliced into pieces
1 cup breadcrumbs
½ cup olive oil
⅓ cup fresh lemon juice
½ cup chicken broth
¼ cup capers
⅓ cup fresh parsley, chopped
Salt to taste
Pepper to taste
8-10 mushroom pieces, sliced

METHOD

Season chicken with salt and pepper.

In a large skillet, heat olive oil. Add chicken (a little at a time) and cook for 3-4 minutes or until browned. Flip and cook the other side until browned.

Remove from heat, and keep aside on a plate.

In the pan, add the lemon juice, stock and capers and bring to a simmer for 5 minutes.

Remove chicken to a serving dish. Add remaining oil to the sauce and whisk vigorously. Pour the sauce over chicken and garnish with parsley.

CASHEW CHICKEN

INGREDIENTS

500 g boneless chicken breasts, cut into small pieces
1 large onion, diced
½ cup coconut milk
¾ cup raw unsalted cashews
2 tbsp tomato paste
1 tbsp ginger garlic paste

METHOD

In a skillet, heat oil, add the ginger garlic paste, onions, chicken, salt and pepper and cook on low flame for 10 minutes until chicken is 70 per cent cooked.

Add the remaining ingredients to a blender and blend until smooth. Pour over the chicken and cook on low flame for 30 minutes.

HOMESTYLE CHICKEN

INGREDIENTS

500 g boneless chicken breasts, cut into pieces
Salt and pepper to taste
2 tsp garlic powder
½ cup grated onion
½ cup tomatoes, pureed
100 g sliced fresh mushrooms
¼ cup butter, melted
1 tbsp fresh lemon juice
1 tsp chopped fresh parsley

METHOD

Preheat the oven to 180°C.

In a bowl, mix together the melted butter, garlic powder, lemon juice, chicken and pepper and keep it for 30 minutes.

Spread mushrooms in an even layer at the bottom of the dish followed by the chicken mixture and topped with mushrooms, onion and tomato puree. Drizzle the remaining butter over the chicken, and sprinkle with parsley.

Bake uncovered for 45 minutes in the preheated oven, until chicken is golden brown and juices run clear.

CHICKEN IN TOMATO GRAVY

INGREDIENTS

300 g boneless chicken breasts, cut into pieces
¼ cup flour
½ tsp salt
1 pinch ground black pepper
3 tbsp butter
100 g tomato puree
½ cup water
Salt to taste
2 tsp chili powder
1 tsp ginger garlic paste

METHOD

In a shallow dish or bowl, combine flour, ½ tsp salt and ground black pepper. Coat chicken breasts with flour mixture. Melt butter in a large skillet over medium heat and brown chicken on all sides. Remove from skillet and drain on paper towels.

In the same skillet, combine the rest of the ingredients and bring to a boil.

Reduce heat, cover and cook for 1 hour or until chicken is tender.

COCONUT CHICKEN CURRY

INGREDIENTS

500 g chicken, cut into pieces
Salt and pepper to taste
2 whole red chillies, stems removed
1 onion, thinly sliced
1 tsp garlic, chopped
½ tsp ginger, chopped
1 tbsp oil
1 tsp garam masala powder
1 can coconut milk
3-4 curry leaves

METHOD

Season chicken pieces with salt and pepper.

Heat oil. Add curry leaves and red whole chillies.

Add onions and garlic and cook for 1 minute.

Add chicken and garam masala, tossing lightly to coat.

Stir in medium heat and cook for 10 minutes.

Pour coconut milk and stir to combine. Cover and cook on simmer, stirring occasionally, approximately for 40 minutes or till chicken is tender.

GARLIC AND ROSEMARY CHICKEN

INGREDIENTS

800 g chicken
Salt and pepper to taste
1 lemon
2 sprigs of rosemary
3 tbsp olive oil
5-6 cloves of garlic, mashed
$1/3$ cup white wine
$1/3$ cup chicken broth

METHOD

Rub the chicken with olive oil, rosemary, lemon juice, salt and pepper and let it marinate for 30 minutes.

Preheat the oven to 160°C. Arrange the chicken, stuff the garlic and butter in the chicken skin and roast for 25 minutes.

In a mixing bowl, whisk together wine and chicken broth. Continue roasting for about 25 minutes longer, or till it turns golden brown and juices run clear.

Note: Baste with pan juices every 10 minutes. Cover with aluminum foil to keep warm and serve after 5 minutes.

Food for Thought:
I always select and prepare my masalas before cooking any dish, whether vegetarian or non-vegetarian.
However, chicken is one ingredient that is versatile and can be cooked with different combinations and variations. Chicken is consumed widely and its importance in your kitchen will always prevail.
No other meat dish has been as internalized as chicken.
After all, there is a
Chicken Soup for the Soul too!

EXTRA VIRGIN OLIVE OIL

Remember This Oil, Forget Alzheimer's

This is the oil extracted from the first press of olives and is the purest form of oil. It contains polyphenols which not only improve learning and memory, but also minimize the age and disease-related changes. The oil also fights against proteins that are toxic to the brain and that induce Alzheimer's.

There are two varieties of olives—green and black. The extra virgin olive oil from the green grape is slightly lighter in taste than the olive oil from the black grape which gives a bitter aftertaste. Nonetheless, extra virgin olive oil, from both the green and the black grapes, is really good for the mind.

It is my favourite type of oil, especially in salads and pastas. The first press of olives gives us extra virgin olive oil and has a lot of flavour. It is also healthy since it doesn't have to be cooked; it loses its properties and flavour when heated. The olive oil experience has been very interesting. I have visited olive oil farms in France and Spain to understand it better, and it will give me much pleasure to take you through these indulgences. I love the extra virgin olive oil that is extracted from black olives. It has an aftertaste which is bitter. The one from green olives doesn't have a bitter aftertaste. You can use it in bread and tomatoes or in pesto. It tastes amazing and is very good for the skin too.

I met a gorgeous woman in Marseille who owned a farm and a store of varieties of olive oils, and it was enough to make a chef like me go crazy. I learnt a lot from her and got loads of bottles back home with me. Another important detail—using extra virgin olive oil in pastas helps in easy digestion.

Nowadays you get a variety of olive oils, for example, the infused olive oils. I find it a very interesting concept— olive oil with basil, with rosemary, chilli and my favourite, garlic infused extra virgin olive oil! Isn't it fascinating? These types of olive oils are meant to be kept on the table to be added as per choice, and they go very well with Italian cuisine!

Having a spoonful of extra virgin olive oil in the morning helps your stomach and keeps your skin beautiful. Well, you can try it, make your own opinion about it and share it with me! Extra virgin olive oil with black olives is my favourite. Though now there are many countries producing olive oil, my favourite still remain the ones from Spain and France.

SUN-DRIED TOMATOES IN OLIVE OIL

INGREDIENTS

2 garlic cloves, crushed
½ cup extra virgin olive oil
100 g sun-dried tomatoes
1 tbsp white wine
¼ cup black olives, pitted
Handful of fresh basil, finely chopped

METHOD

Preheat oven to 200°C.

Pour the olive oil into a large skillet and add all the ingredients in it.

Transfer it into a glass jar and you can enjoy it after keeping it in the sun for 2 days.

PESTO

INGREDIENTS

1 cup basil
½ cup extra virgin olive oil
¼ cup pine nuts
Salt and pepper to taste
1 tsp lemon juice

METHOD

Blend everything together in a blender till smooth.

Adjust seasoning and add olive oil for consistency.

OLIVE OIL CAKE

INGREDIENTS

150 ml extra virgin olive oil
150 g castor sugar
140 g brown sugar
1 tsp vanilla essence
1 lemon zest
2 eggs
1 tbsp milk
150 g plain flour
A pinch of salt
1 tsp bicarbonate of soda

METHOD

Mix together the olive oil, sugars, vanilla and lemon zest. Add the eggs and milk, and mix well. Then add flour, salt and baking powder, all sifted together, and continue mixing slowly in the shape of 8 so that the batter is light and fluffy.

Preheat the oven to 180°C.

Transfer the batter into a greased mould.

Bake for 45 minutes. Enjoy it when it is warm.

STRAWBERRY AND WALNUT SALAD

INGREDIENTS

Serves 4-6
½ cup extra virgin olive oil
5-6 leaves of iceberg lettuce, washed
3½ tbsp fresh lemon juice
½-1 tsp whole black peppercorns, crushed
4-5 strawberries
6-7 walnuts, broken
¼ cup feta cheese

METHOD

In a bowl, add lettuce, strawberries and walnuts.

In another bowl, mix olive oil, lemon juice and pepper to make the dressing.

Drizzle over the salad and add feta cheese on top. Serve immediately.

OLIVE OIL BREAD

INGREDIENTS

15 g fresh yeast
500 g flour, plus extra for dusting
2 tsp salt
1 tsp sugar
2 tbsp olive oil

METHOD

In a mixing bowl, add the flour, salt and sugar. Mix and then make a well in the centre of the flour and add yeast, warm water (approx 100 ml) and olive oil.

Mix quickly with your hands or a wooden spoon to make a soft and sticky dough. Wipe the dough around the bowl to pick up any loose flour.

Sprinkle the work surface with flour. Knead by stretching it away from yourself with your hand, then folding it towards yourself and pushing it away, and repeat the process.

When the dough is smooth, put it back into the mixing bowl, cover with a towel and leave to rest for 1 hour or till it doubles in size.

Knead the dough and shape it into a ball. Place it on an oiled baking sheet and lightly cut on top with a sharp knife. Cover for 30 minutes. Preheat oven to 220°C and bake for 30-35 minutes until golden brown and crisp.

Food for Thought:
Olives and extra virgin olive oil are exotic ingredients and the best way to consume them is in salads, soups, appetizers and with bread.
Eating olives is one of the ways of healthy living!
Extra virgin olive oil is popular because of both its taste and various nutritious qualities.
If diamonds are forever for women, olives are forever for chefs and cuisines.

AVOCADO

Untangle Your Brain

Avocado is an incredible fruit. It is not native to India and, in fact, has recently been introduced and gained popularity quickly because of its taste, and of course, immense health benefits. As avocado is native to South Central Mexico, it is best used in Mexican cuisine. And that reminds me to ask you something—have you tried guacamole? If not, I insist you do, as you will fall in love with this dip.

Avocado contains both vitamin K and foliate, and helps in preventing blood clots in the brain as well as improves cognitive functions, especially memory and concentration. They're also rich in vitamin B and vitamin C which aren't stored in your body and need to be replenished daily. Plus, they have the highest protein and lowest sugar content than any fruit. Here is a closer look at how avocados protect brain health.

As a mono-saturated fat, the avocado can lower blood pressure and increase blood flow—two factors that can reduce the risk of cognitive decline. Monounsaturated fats can also prevent insulin resistance and fight type-2 diabetes, which is another risk factor for Alzheimer's.

High in foliate, avocados are thought to prevent the formation of the brain tangles which are said to cause Alzheimer's.

Avocados, having a high amount of potassium, omega-3 and oleic acid, can reduce blood pressure, and a lower blood pressure has been shown to be beneficial for brain health. The amount of potassium is more than that found in bananas. Avocados and avocado oil are high in monounsaturated oleic acid, a 'heart healthy' fatty acid.

Although admittedly high in fat, avocados are a strong source of omega-3 fatty acids which have been shown to prevent and slow down Alzheimer's. Avocados also have anti-inflammatory properties which fight Alzheimer's.

Avocados also boast of vitamin K. Vitamin K improves blood flow, decreases risk of strokes and may also prevent Alzheimer's. Other than the above, avocado is loaded with healthy fats, fibre and various important nutrients. Guacamole is one of my favourite dips and you must check some of my easy and yummy avocado recipes on Shipra's Kitchen online!

AVOCADO SUSHI

INGREDIENTS

½ cup brown rice
3 tbsp rice vinegar
A pinch of salt
1 tsp honey
½ cup cucumber, cut into strips
1 avocado, cut into strips
4 nori sheets

METHOD

Place brown rice in boiled water and then reduce heat and simmer until cooked.

In a small bowl, mix vinegar, honey and salt.

Gradually, pour the mixture over quinoa and mix well.

Spread the rice on each sushi sheet, leaving 2" space on the sides.

Place cucumber and avocado on top. Roll up tightly and cut into rolls.

AVOCADO ROLLS

INGREDIENTS

2 tsp olive oil
¼ cup diced onions
1 cup sliced white button mushrooms
1 small garlic clove, finely minced
2 eggs
Salt to taste
2 turns black pepper, freshly ground
½ small avocado, skin removed and chopped
6 phyllo sheets
½ cup butter

METHOD

Sauté garlic, onion and mushrooms in olive oil until softened, for about 5 minutes.

In a small bowl, whisk eggs and pour over the mixture. Add salt and pepper. Stir constantly until eggs are cooked. Add salt and pepper to taste.

Scoop on a plate and mix in avocado. Let it cool at room temperature.

Layer a phyllo sheet, grease it evenly with butter, then layer another sheet. Brush it with butter and repeat with all 6 sheets. After topping the last sheet with butter, place the avocado mix 2" from the border and roll it to make a perfect roll. Seal the ends with butter. Bake in an oven preheated to 200° C for 10 minutes. Serve hot.

NACHOS WITH GUACAMOLE

INGREDIENTS

2 avocados, skinned and mashed
2 tbsp lemon juice
Salt to taste
1 tbsp chopped coriander leaves
2-3 jalapenos
1 onion
1 tomato
2 chillies, finely chopped

METHOD

Combine all the ingredients in a food processor or blender.

After that, add a little lime or lemon juice—a splash of acidity to balance the richness of the avocado.

Add chopped coriander, chillies, onion and tomato.

Serve with nachos.

BLUEBERRY AND AVOCADO SMOOTHIE

INGREDIENTS

100 g blueberries
20 g avocado
20 g banana
2 tsp chia seeds
½ cup pomegranate juice
2-3 cubes of ice

METHOD

Place all ingredients in blender. Blend until smooth.
   Serve chilled.

AVOCADO SANDWICH

INGREDIENTS

1 egg, beaten
1 avocado, pitted and sliced
Salt and pepper to taste
2 slices multigrain bread
1 tbsp cream cheese

METHOD

In a bowl, mix avocado, salt and pepper to taste.
   In a saucepan, boil water, drop the egg and poach it. Sieve and keep aside.
   On a slice of bread, spread the cream cheese evenly. Place avocado and eggs and sandwich it.
   Slice and serve.

BARLEY SALAD

INGREDIENTS

½ cup cooked barley
1 cup bean sprouts
Salt and pepper to taste
1 small ripe avocado, peeled, pitted and diced

FOR LEMONY YOGURT SAUCE

½ cup plain yogurt
1 tsp grated lemon zest
1 tsp lemon juice
1 tbsp chopped chives
A pinch of kosher salt

METHOD

In a bowl, mix everything together.

Food for Thought:
The guacamole recipe is my favourite. Since avocado is a high-fibre fruit and has no taste of its own, adding lemon juice, salt and pepper or smoked paprika is the best way to consume it. Tasty and healthy! Another great ingredient with a long history, it was consumed across classes and countries. Through this special ingredient adorned the tables of all the princes, bishops and people of consequence, it was also consumed by all and sundry.

BEETROOT

More Power to the Brain

I am now introducing recipes with a gorgeous-coloured vegetable—beetroot—which is also a complete source of energy. It is one of the ingredients that can be had either raw or boiled or juiced. In every form it is going to taste delicious. In fact, you can mix any other vegetables and fruits with beetroot, and it will still give its own unique flavour and taste, and make the dish more delicious. The root vegetable beta vulgaris rubra, which is popularly known as red beetroot, has grabbed a lot of attention for its health benefits and has become an important functional food in our diet.

Beetroot originally belonged to Europe and was initially cultivated by the Romans. This is one of the vegetables that offers nutrients from both its roots and leaves. It requires muddy, moist and thick soil for proper growth. It is a vegetable that one should make a part of one's daily diet. There are no side effects of eating this vegetable; by all means it will only have a positive effect on your body. Of course, being high on sugar, it is not recommended to diabetic patients, and because of high sugar, it is used to extract sucrose from the beet plant. This beautiful vegetable is highly beneficial in increasing haemoglobin in the human body and is recommended to be consumed regularly.

Beetroot juice helps to detoxify the body and proves to be a great purifier. It also helps to build stamina and stimulate red blood cell production. Though it is high in sugar, it can help you to keep your weight down as it is low in calories and almost fat-free. Including this vegetable in your diet is the most nutritious way of losing weight.

As per studies, beetroot contains nitrates that produce nitric oxide. This is a type of gas that helps to relax and strengthen blood vessels which improves blood flow and pressure. It also reduces heart strokes. Beetroot is rich in fibres and minerals like manganese, potassium and iron that help to maintain good health. Beetroot is the best natural home remedy for all hair problems. The juice of beetroot helps to reduce stress, which, in turn, reduces your hair fall. While preparing beetroot juice, make sure you add carrot, lettuce and spinach to make it more nutritious.

Beetroot comes with a lot of medicinal values. It helps to prevent terrible diseases like liver cancer and colon cancer. It is not called your 'liver's best friend' for nothing.

Beetroot is the best solution for people whose mental power is declining with age. It helps to increase the blood flow to the brain, thus reducing the effect of dementia.

There are various ways to have beetroot on your dining table. You can steam, boil, roast or can also consume it raw. These days, chefs keep experimenting with new recipes and so beetroot can be used in your regular food and salads.

Well, beetroot is one of the ingredients which my grandma always told me to have; she said, 'Your cheeks will become bright and red and you will not require any make-up when you grow up, Shipra.' Little did I understand then but now I do. As beetroot is said to be good for increasing the haemoglobin level, it makes you look healthy and pretty. I do like beetroot in many forms—boiled, juiced or mixed with other vegetables, and so I am sharing some recipes with you which will make you fall in love with this beautiful and healthy ingredient which is good for all ages. But, do check with your doctor in case you have any disease or a specific allergy.

This root vegetable is amazing when fried into chips as well!

BEET CARPACCIO RECIPE

INGREDIENTS

2 cooked beetroot, thinly sliced
1 tbsp extra-virgin olive oil
2 tbsp fresh orange juice
2 tsp white wine vinegar
½ tsp orange zest
Salt and black pepper to taste
1 tbsp chives, finely chopped

METHOD

In a plate, place beetroot slices.
Season to taste.
In a large bowl, combine vinegar, orange juice, zest, salt, pepper and olive oil.
Drizzle the dressing on top of the beetroot.
Sprinkle with chives on top of the salad and serve.

BEET CARROT GINGER JUICE

INGREDIENTS

2 beetroots
2 cups carrot
1 apple, cored and peeled
¼" fresh ginger
½ tsp lemon juice

METHOD

Take the juice out by adding the ingredients to the juicer.

BEETROOT KEBAB

INGREDIENTS

1 cup beetroot, boiled
2 potatoes, boiled and mashed
½ tsp ginger garlic paste
1 tbsp amchoor powder
A pinch of chaat masala
Salt to taste
½ cup crushed oats, to coat
Oil

METHOD

In a bowl, mix the beetroot, potatoes, salt, chaat masala, ginger garlic paste and amchoor powder.
Make round balls and flatten them.
Coat the kebabs with crushed oats.
In a flat pan, heat the oil and lightly fry these.
Serve with green chutney.

BEETROOT SOUP

INGREDIENTS

2 beetroots
1 onion, peeled
4-5 cloves of garlic
¼" ginger
2 tomatoes
1 tsp salt
1 tsp pepper
1 potato
½ ltr water

METHOD

In a skillet, add all the ingredients along with ½ ltr of water. Cover and boil for 20 minutes.

Strain and keep the broth.

Chop the beetroot and add to the clear broth, adjust seasoning and serve hot.

SIMPLY BEETROOT

INGREDIENTS

2-3 beetroots, boiled and chopped
1 tbsp oil
1 tbsp mustard seeds
10-12 curry leaves
½ cup chopped onions
1 tsp chopped ginger
2 split green chillies

METHOD

In a kadhai, heat oil, mustard seeds, curry leaves, onions, ginger and split green chillies.

Sauté the beetroot and the spices together.

Mix well and simmer for 5 minutes. Serve.

BEETROOT MILKSHAKE

INGREDIENTS

2 beetroots, boiled, peeled and cut
125 ml milk, chilled
2 scoops vanilla ice cream

METHOD

In a blender, puree the beetroot. Add milk and crushed ice and blend. Add vanilla ice cream and mix. Serve chilled.

Food for Thought:
Beetroot juice with apple and carrot, popularly known as ABC, is a great combination of fruit and vegetable juice. I love adding this vegetable to my soups and curries to give them a beautiful colour and of course, to make the recipe healthier at the same time. When I was a child, my grandmother used to run after me to feed me beetroot in one way or the other, whenever it was in season, and I used to run away from it. I always camouflage it when feeding it to my children to escape the drill, which is of course the way to deal with this smart new generation!

COCONUT OIL

Fighting Bad Bacteria, Fighting Memory Loss

In ancient India, the use of coconut oil was extensive as it has medicinal properties and helps in healing. Coconut oil is also considered as 'superfood' due to its countless benefits. It is excellent for the human body as it is a rich source of saturated fat. It consists of fatty acids with medicinal properties. The main element of coconut oil is lauric acid which is also the main element of milk fat. Lauric acid helps to improve the immune system of the body. It helps to reduce cholesterol and can help to prevent heart diseases.

Coconut oil helps to burn more fat and is an important factor in fighting obesity—one of the biggest health problems in today's world. It contains short and medium-chain fatty acids that help in shedding excessive weight.

Hence, people living in tropical coastal areas, who use coconut oil every day as their primary cooking oil, are normally not fat, obese or overweight.

Other than this, coconut oil can be used to maintain beauty and also helps in anti-ageing. It is for this reason that many of the cosmetic brands are producing skin and hair products containing coconut oil. This oil helps to enhance sensitive skin and cures cracked lips, sunburn and diaper rashes. If used as a face oil, it will protect the skin from UV damage.

Calcium is an important component of our teeth. Since coconut oil facilitates absorption of calcium by the body, it helps in developing strong teeth. It also stops tooth decay. Recent research suggests that coconut oil is beneficial in reducing plaque formation and plaque induced gingivitis.

Candida, also known as systemic candidiasis, is a disease caused from excessive and uncontrolled growth of a type of yeast called candida albicans in the stomach. Coconut provides relief from the inflammation caused by candida, both externally and internally. Its high moisture retaining capacity keeps the skin from cracking or peeling off.

When applied to infected areas, coconut oil forms a chemical layer that protects the infected body part from dust, air, fungi, bacteria and viruses. Coconut oil is highly effective on **bruises** because it speeds up the healing process of damaged tissues.

It is believed that coconut oil plays an instrumental role in reducing the viral susceptibility of HIV and cancer patients. It also helps in preventing liver diseases because it is easily converted into energy when it reaches the liver, thus reducing the workload of the liver and also preventing accumulation of fat.

Coconut oil also relieves one from stress and its antioxidant properties reduce blood sugar. As mentioned earlier, coconut oil improves the ability of our body to absorb important minerals.

Coconut oil is often used by athletes, bodybuilders and by those who are dieting. What makes it a favourite among them is that it contains less calories than other oils, its fat content is easily converted into energy, and it does not lead to accumulation of fat in the heart and arteries.

Coconut oil is far easier to digest than the other edible oils and is thus suitable for digestive disorders. It can improve your metabolism and maintain energy level. In today's times, there are different kinds of coconut oil and different terms are used to label them. It is very important to understand them as it will help you select the best oil according to your requirements.

Organic: The coconuts used to produce this type of oil are not exposed to pesticides while they are growing. Normally, these products are inspected and certified.

All-natural: Natural oil is manufactured without using any type of chemical in its production process.

Refined: The natural oil is processed further where the coconut flavour and all the impurities are removed.

Cold-pressed: This is the method of extracting oil from

either dry or fresh coconuts.

The moment you add coconut oil to popular foods like baked items, sautéed veggies or seared meats, it gives the dish a unique flavour. Flavoured oil makes a huge difference to the food by giving it a distinct taste.

I remember the South Indian dishes cooked by one of my aunts from South India. She used to smell of coconut oil and it was such a pleasure to be around her. Of course, another reason was that she cooked extremely well and she was the reason why I fell in love with this beautiful oil. Flavour, taste and health benefits of coconut oil, including increased energy, weight loss, natural antibiotic activity, cholesterol reduction and insulin stabilization, have been substantiated by scientific research world over. Coconut oil is healthy to the body but should not be had in huge quantities. Here are some recipes that require a little coconut oil and will improve your health with every bite.

With so many benefits how can it not be considered a 'SUPERFOOD'!

VEGETABLES IN COCONUT CURRY

INGREDIENTS

1 tbsp coconut oil
1 can of coconut milk
2 cups broccoli, carrots and cauliflower, blanched
1 cup bell peppers, diced
1 onion, diced
Salt and black pepper to taste
1 tsp minced garlic
1 tsp lime juice

METHOD

In a pan, heat coconut oil. Add vegetables and sauté for 2 minutes on high flame.

Add onion and garlic and cook for 1 minute, and then, add coconut milk and lime.

Cover and cook for 5 minutes and serve.

COCONUT CRUSTED SALMON

INGREDIENTS

½ cup desiccated coconut
Salt to taste
500 g salmon, skinned and sliced into 4 pieces
1 egg, beaten
1 tbsp coconut oil

METHOD

Preheat oven to 375°C.

Mix the shredded coconut and salt together in a shallow bowl. Set aside.

Dip the salmon in the egg and coat both sides with the coconut mixture. Lay it flat on a sheet pan. Brush generously with coconut oil.

Bake the salmon for 15-20 minutes, flipping once, until the salmon is cooked and the coconut crust is slightly browned and crisp. Serve warm.

Serve with paprika sauce.

COCONUT OIL BANANA CHIPS

INGREDIENTS

2 tbsp coconut oil
2 raw bananas, sliced lengthwise
Mixed masalas (1 tsp salt + 1 tsp chilli powder + mango powder)

METHOD

Heat oil and fry the chips until golden brown in colour.
Toss in the prepared masala, mix and keep it in an airtight container.

STRAWBERRY AND ASPARAGUS SALAD IN COCONUT OIL

INGREDIENTS

2 tbsp coconut oil
3-4 asparagus, trimmed and blanched
5-6 strawberries
1 cup baby spinach
1 ½ tsp lemon juice
½ cup walnuts
Salt and pepper to taste

METHOD

Melt coconut oil in a skillet over medium heat. Stir in salt, pepper and lemon juice and make a dressing. Transfer into a bottle.

In a large bowl, mix the rest of the ingredients and then drizzle the prepared coconut oil dressing.

Dress with walnuts and serve.

STIR-FRIED COCONUT CHICKEN

INGREDIENTS

500 g boneless chicken, cut into cubes
2" ginger juliennes
2 tbsp coconut oil
2 tsp minced garlic
1 tsp fish sauce
1 tsp soya sauce
1 cup spring onions, chopped (green and white part)
Pepper and salt to taste

METHOD

In a wok, heat the coconut oil until the oil is melted and hot.

Add ginger and stir for 20 seconds.

Then, add onions and sauté for 20 seconds.

Now add chicken and the sauces, salt and pepper to taste. Cook and stir for 2 minutes.

Cover and cook the chicken for 2 minutes until the chicken is tender.

Remove the cover and cook on high flame until the sauce sticks to the chicken. Serve hot.

PANCAKES

INGREDIENTS

2 tsp coconut oil, melted
2 bananas, mashed until smooth
2 eggs
½ cup wheat flour
½ cup milk
½ tsp butter
¼ tsp baking soda
½ tsp ground cinnamon
A pinch of salt
¼ cup walnuts, chopped

METHOD

In a food processor, add bananas, eggs, baking soda, salt, flour and cinnamon, and beat until batter is smooth and fluffy.

Now heat a non-stick pan, and pour a ladle full of the batter.

Cook until bubbles form (approximately 3 to 4 minutes). Flip and cook until browned on the other side for approximately 3 minutes on low flame. Repeat with remaining batter, greasing the pan with coconut oil before pouring the batter.

Sprinkle walnuts on top and serve.

Food for Thought:
Desiccated coconut, fresh coconut, coconut milk, coconut water and coconut oil—these are some forms of coconut that we consume. Isn't it amazing that one fruit can give you so much of variety? I simply love the way coconut smells. Coconut is used in making chutneys, vegetables, meat and fish curries, desserts, etc. and there is a lot more that can be prepared from this amazing fruit. Coconut water is the best cooling drink to have in any season, especially in summers and is also good for those who are on a diet. We are lucky to have coconuts so easily available to us in India!

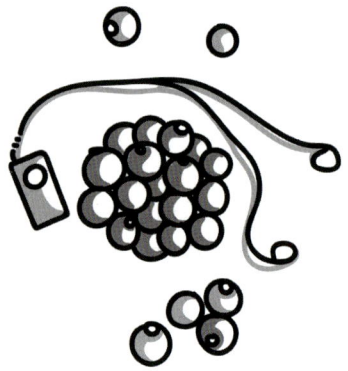

BLUEBERRY

Berry! To Beat the Blue

Blueberry is one of the highest antioxidant-rich foods known to man. They are rich in vitamin C, vitamin K and fibre. Because of their high levels of gallic acid, blueberries are especially beneficial for protecting our brains from degeneration and stress.

Various types of berries come in different seasons, and berries like strawberry, mulberry, gooseberry, raspberry and blueberry are really popular. Just the thought of them makes your mouth water and I am sure everyone in this world has their favourite berry!

Let's talk about blueberries. They are a treat to have during summers. They are filled with nutrients and can be either eaten fresh or incorporated in different recipes.

Blueberries are good for bones as they are rich in phosphorous, calcium, iron, vitamin K and zinc. They help in strengthening the built and structure of the bone. Yes, a soft fruit can give strength to your bones and this is the beautiful magic of nature. Blueberries contain potassium, sodium, magnesium and calcium, which help to decrease blood pressure naturally.

Eating this delicious fruit will help to reduce the risk of different types of cancer as well. They also help in keeping the urinary tract healthy. Blueberries come with anti-ageing properties. Studies have shown that blueberries protect the brain from oxidative stress and also help to reduce age-related conditions such as Alzheimer's disease or dementia. And yes, eating these blueberries will improve short and long-term memory. Additionally, research has shown that they support cardiovascular health too.

Blueberries are the best choice to improve your daily diet. Here are some tips on how you can use it in your daily food.

Natural lutein in blueberries can boost night vision and help in slowing down age-related vision loss. They also work effectively to slow down cataracts and muscular degeneration.

You can put them either on muffins or pancakes. You can also add them in the breakfast cereal bowl with reduced milk and nuts. This is also an important ingredient for weight loss. Let me also tell you that half a cup of blueberries equals to a single serving of fruit.

Blueberries are superfoods (food with health benefits) that will help you better your health and life.

Blueberries are sweet and tart in taste. They are high

in nutrition, yet low in calories. Normally, the best time to have them is from May till October. This is the time they are in season. This fruit is native to North America and there is an integrated history to it. Blueberries were important crops in colonial America. The Americans used to gather blueberries, dry them under the summer's sun and store them during winters. During the Civil War, a beverage was made which was a very important staple for soldiers.

Here is some storage information on blueberries. When you buy blueberries, you will have to refrigerate them. Also, ensure you do not freeze them and it is advisable to consume them within a couple of days after buying. Keep the blueberries in a container and do not wash them until they are soft enough to eat.

Many desserts and other dishes are prepared from blueberries. In fact, blueberry jam is very famous for breakfast and can be easily prepared at home as well. In this book, I have come up with interesting recipes that you will not only enjoy eating but cooking too. They are not at all time-consuming and are very easy to prepare.

BLUEBERRY JUICE

INGREDIENTS

1 cup blueberries, fresh or frozen
½ cup red port wine
2 cups water
1 tsp pure vanilla essence
A pinch of salt
¼ cup blueberries, boiled

METHOD

Add all the ingredients to a blender until smooth.

Strain the mixture and keep the juice.

Now peel the skin of the boiled blueberries, add into the juice and serve chilled.

BLUEBERRY PIZZA

INGREDIENTS

11" pizza crust, ready-made
100 g blueberry filling
¼ cup butter, melted
2 tbsp brown sugar
1 tsp vanilla essence
50 g cream cheese, softened

METHOD

Preheat oven to 180° C.

Mix melted butter with a drop of vanilla and brush over the entire pizza crust.

Bake crust for about 5 minutes or until golden brown, then allow crust to cool.

Blend together cream cheese, butter and vanilla essence until light and fluffy. Add brown sugar and mix well.

Carefully spread cream cheese mixture evenly over pizza crust.

Add an even layer of blueberry filling and let the pizza cool.

BLUEBERRY SALAD

INGREDIENTS

1 cup blueberries
Salt to taste
¼ tsp paprika
1 orange, peeled and skin removed
1 tsp balsamic vinegar
2 tbsp extra virgin olive oil
2 tbsp blueberry juice
1 tsp lemon juice
1 cup baby spinach
20 g ricotta cheese, crumbled

METHOD

In a bowl, combine olive oil, salt, paprika, lemon juice, blueberry juice and vinegar.

In another bowl, add blueberries, spinach and oranges.

Drizzle the prepared dressing.

Toss and serve, dressed with ricotta cheese.

BLUEBERRY TACOS

INGREDIENTS

100 g blueberry filling
100 ml whipping cream

FOR TACO SHELLS

1 cup olive oil for brushing
5-6 tortilla sheets
¼ cup granulated sugar
1 tsp ground cinnamon

METHOD

In a bowl, whip the cream with a hand blender until it holds soft peaks. Transfer into a piping bag and refrigerate.

FOR TACO SHELLS

In a bowl, combine sugar and cinnamon.
Brush oil evenly on each tortilla, fold it into half and bake in an oven preheated to 180°C for 20 minutes or until light golden in colour.
When the taco shell is golden brown, carefully lift and remove it from the oven.
To assemble tacos: Divide the pie filling evenly among the taco shells, and top with whipped cream.

BLUEBERRY PIE

INGREDIENTS

FOR THE FILLING

¾ cup sugar
¼ tsp cinnamon
2 cups fresh blueberries
1 tsp lemon juice

FOR THE PIE CRUST

1 cup flour
½ cup almond powder
1 cup butter, chilled
1 tsp sugar
½ cup milk
2 egg yolks
1 tsp vanilla essence

METHOD

FOR THE FILLING

In a pan, combine sugar, ½ cup water, cinnamon, lemon juice and blueberries. Cook while stirring until the blueberries start to soften and the sauce becomes thick. Cool and then chill in the refrigerator.

FOR THE CRUST

Combine the flour, sugar, butter and almond powder in the bowl with your hands till it looks like breadcrumbs.

Add cold water to form dough. Chill the dough.

Now flatten the dough with a rolling pin carefully and slowly.

Now place it in the pie mould and flatten with fingertips, covering the mould till the edges. Prick with a fork.

Cover with foil and bake at 180°C for 10-13 minutes.

In a bowl, combine milk, eggs and vanilla essence with a fork and keep aside.

Now add the filling and the egg mixture and bake for 10 minutes or until the filling sets.

Take it out of the oven and let it cool at room temperature.

Then refrigerate.

BLUEBERRY OATS BARS

INGREDIENTS

1 cup frozen blueberries
1 tbsp honey
¼ tsp vanilla extract
A pinch of salt
½ tsp cornstarch
1 cup dried oats

METHOD

In a saucepan, combine the blueberries, oats, water, honey, vanilla extract, and a pinch of salt. Mix cornstarch in 2 tbsp water and mix evenly.

Bring to a boil, then let it simmer until thickened.

Chill in the refrigerator.

Cut into pieces and enjoy!

Food for Thought:
I preserve blueberries by making jams, which, of course, can be consumed in any season. All you have to do is add a little water and sugar and let it reduce till the jam consistency is fine. Yeah, it's that simple! It tastes good in smoothies, shakes, desserts and sauces as well, especially with meat!

Chef Phillippe in Chamonix prepared the best blueberry tart I had ever eaten in my life. I guess the reason was that he had made the tart with freshly-plucked blueberries. I still can't forget the taste. I always use fresh and seasonal fruits or vegetables as the taste is incomparable and a lot of chefs across the world prefer to do so too.

BONE BROTH

A Healthy Belly, a Healthier Mind

Bone broth goes back to ancient cultures across the world. It has been used as a remedy for the sick as it has a lot of healing properties. It has high levels of collagen that helps to reduce intestinal inflammation, and healing amino acids like proline and glycine keep your immune system functioning properly. And bone broth finds a place in our superfoods as it also helps to improve memory.

Bone broth is made with animal bones. Cartilage found in animal joint areas, such as in chicken feet, beef or lamb knuckles, trachea and ribs, hooves and skin, tend to yield the most nutritious broth. It is cooked and simmered for a very long time and is an ancient recipe for curing cold and flu. In India, it is popularly known as 'kharoron ka soup' or 'paye ka soup'. The idea is to extract gelatin (cartilage), bone marrow, amino acids and minerals from the animal bones and sieve. That's how you prepare the bone broth. Naturally, it contains all the nutrients. After 12–14 hours of simmering the soup, retain the liquid and discard the bones.

Bone broth is rich in collagen. It also releases minerals from bones. The basic and the most popular 'brown sauce' is also made with bones and, of course, consuming it is really healthy, whether in the form of soup or in curries. Collagen is also an important component of the muscles, tendons, ligaments, blood vessels and bones. It also improves the skin, promotes wound and injury healing, protects connective tissue and strengthens bone cartilage.

I love consuming bone broth. I'm listing its benefits below, after reading which you will look forward to drinking bone broth too.

Firstly, bone broth is loaded with vital nutrients like magnesium, calcium, zinc and iron. It helps in healing the gut and promoting immunity.

Secondly, since bone broth is very easy to digest, it helps with other digestive disorders as well, which I guess is really common nowadays.

Thirdly, bone broth contains glutamine, chondroitin sulphate and other compounds which help to prevent osteoarthritis and prove healthy for joints. It prevents inflammatory bowel disease, leaky gut syndrome and has an anti-inflammatory effect. It may also improve blood circulation and support digestion by enhancing stomach acid secretion.

Fourthly, drinking bone broth keeps the bones stronger. It helps in improving sleep disorders, like insomnia, irritability, fatigue and anxiety. It helps in improving memory as well.

Fifthly, it is most recommended to have it in the form of soup as it keeps you healthy and is comforting. Bone broth promotes strength and nourishment, especially in times of sickness, injury, rehabilitation, and helps to prevent bone and connective tissue disorders.

Lastly, it is a completely natural solution for healthy skin, hair and nails and keeps you glowing in all seasons.

Now let's talk about how to store it.
It can be stored in the refrigerator but not for more than a week. You can also freeze it in the ice cube trays and use the frozen cubes as and when required.

Here are a few recipes that you can try and share your views!

LEMON CORIANDER CHICKEN NOODLES SOUP

INGREDIENTS

1 cup chicken bone broth
Salt and pepper to taste
Garlic powder
¼ cup boiled noodles
½ tsp lemon
1 egg, beaten
1 tsp fresh coriander, chopped
½ cup chicken, boiled and shredded
For thickening
1 tbsp cornflour
3 tbsp water

METHOD

In a skillet, add the chicken broth, garlic, lemon juice, salt and pepper and boil for 3-4 minutes.

Add boiled chicken and coriander. Boil further for a minute, then drop in the beaten egg and stir. Now add the boiled noodles.

Add the cornflour and water mixture in it and boil till it thickens slightly.

Serve hot.

CHICKEN PULAO

INGREDIENTS

2 tbsp oil
½ medium-sized onion, sliced
1 tbsp ginger garlic paste
1 tsp chilli powder
1 tsp garam masala
1 cup basmati rice (soaked for an hour)
3-4 slit green chillies
Salt to taste
500 g chicken
2 cups chicken born broth

METHOD

Heat the oil in a skillet.

Sauté onions for a minute.

Add ginger garlic paste and sauté for 2 minutes.

Add chicken, rice, salt, chilli powder, garam masala and chillies along with the broth.

Cook for 20 minutes covered on medium flame or until the rice and chicken are cooked.

CHICKEN CASSEROLE

INGREDIENTS

¼ cup oil
1 onion, chopped
1 cup carrots, chopped
Salt and pepper to taste
1 tsp garlic, minced
1 cup peas
1 kg chicken
1 cup white rice
2 cups chicken bone broth

METHOD

Heat oil in a skillet, add and sauté the onion, garlic, carrot, salt and pepper and cook for 1 minute.

Put the vegetables along with the rest of the ingredients (you may add some water if required).

Cover and cook for 30-35 minutes until rice and chicken are cooked.

CHICKEN STROGANOFF

INGREDIENTS

1 kg chicken, cut into strips
2 tbsp olive oil
1 onion, sliced
1 cup mushrooms, sliced
2 cups chicken bone broth
1 cup cream
½ cup mushrooms, pureed
1 tbsp garlic, minced
Salt and pepper to taste
250 g mushrooms

METHOD

In a skillet, add olive oil and add onions and garlic. Sauté for a minute, then add salt and pepper and cook for a minute.

Now add chicken and flour and sauté for 2-3 minutes.

Add flour and cook further for 2 minutes until light brown in colour.

Add mushroom puree, broth and cook for 10 minutes.

Now add cream and mushrooms and adjust seasoning.

Cook covered for 10-15 minutes until chicken is tender.

Serve hot.

HOMESTYLE MUTTON CURRY

INGREDIENTS

2 cups meat, cut in chunks
2 tbsp ginger garlic paste
2 tbsp oil
2 cups mutton bone broth
2-3 red whole chillies, broken into halves
Salt to taste
1 tsp turmeric powder
2 tsp garam masala

METHOD

In a skillet, add oil and sauté mutton chunks for 3-4 minutes.

Now add garlic and ginger paste and sauté further for 2-3 minutes. Then add red chilies.

Add broth, salt, turmeric, garam masala and cook covered on low flame for 40 minutes or until mutton is tender.

Serve hot with roti or rice.

Food for Thought:
Nowadays with increasing stress and quantum of alcohol consumption, detoxification centres are gaining popularity. Interestingly, broths are useful in fasting and cleansing programs. During fasting, because little or no food or energy source is consumed, protein tissues, like muscles, often break down. Hence consuming bone broth limits or prevents degeneration and helps in the detoxification process.

Whether or not you are on detoxification, my recommendation is to include bone broth in your daily diet to keep problems at bay!

BROCCOLI

The 'Cool' Vegetable

In recent times, broccoli has become very famous worldwide and is extensively used in almost all the dishes, right from starters to the main course. Broccoli existed during the Roman Empire and it is still enjoyed today.

Here is why you should have broccoli in your diet. This amazing food has low sugar and helps you lose weight. Broccoli is said to even prevent and fight cancer.

Broccoli is a green vegetable that looks like a cauliflower and is from the cabbage family. It is mostly green in colour but is also rarely found in purple colour. Broccoli is a rich source of vitamin C, vitamin K, carotenoid compounds and many minerals. It is a powerhouse of nutrients and has numerous health benefits. Broccoli has the chemicals which act as antioxidants and are said to prevent cancer.

It is one of the best detox foods. Broccoli has a lot of soluble fibre which helps in reducing cholesterol from the body. It helps to maintain blood sugar and is good for your heart. It is a perfect food for people on diet. If you are following a diet that includes high amount of meat, dairy and eggs, then adding broccoli will provide nutrients, vitamins, minerals and fibre.

Broccoli is an incredible food that will give you nutrition and also help you maintain your weight. The following nutrients are found in broccoli: vitamins A, B-6, C and E, calcium, manganese, zinc, magnesium, copper, selenium foliate and choline.

The best way to have broccoli is to cook it as little as possible so that you get the maximum nutrition. You can steam or roast it for a few minutes but cooking it for a longer time may destroy its valuable nutrients.

Here is how you can add broccoli to the meal and make it healthy. Broccoli is a complete food that can either be eaten raw, cooked or in soup. You can either make an omelette on a platter or it can be part of a side dish of a main course. Due to its vibrant colour, it makes the meal look exciting and fun.

Kids seldom find broccoli pleasing to their eyes. In order to make your children consume it, it is important to make it interesting for them. All mothers have to go through the stress of coming up with interesting recipes which can be prepared using nutritional ingredients for their children, and this job becomes more taxing in case of fussy children (more on this in my next book, *Foods for Fussy Kids*).

The key to get your child to eat broccoli is to make it interesting every time you serve it to them. For example, in case your kid does not like to eat broccoli in a salad, you can boil it or roast it in soup.

After travelling to different parts of the world, I have worked on a few recipes with broccoli that you might appreciate. At the same time, I have also kept in mind to keep the recipes as simple and quick to prepare as I can.

GARLIC BROCCOLI

INGREDIENTS

1 flower broccoli, cut into florets
1 tbsp butter
1 tsp garlic, minced
1 tsp red pepper flakes
Salt to taste

METHOD

Mix the butter, minced garlic, red pepper flakes and salt.

Add broccoli and marinate for 20 minutes.

Cook in a wok for 2 minutes on high flame and then cover and cook until broccoli is tender.

CREAMY TANDOORI BROCCOLI

INGREDIENTS

1 broccoli, cut into florets
1 tsp white pepper
2 tbsp cream
Salt to taste
1 tsp cardamom powder

METHOD

Mix everything together and marinate broccoli for 20 minutes.

Heat the tandoor and cook the broccoli for 10 minutes or until tender and slightly brown.

Serve hot.

BROCCOLI BIRYANI

INGREDIENTS

1 broccoli, cut into florets
1 cup basmati rice, soaked for an hour
2 tbsp ghee
1 bay leaf
Salt to taste
1" ginger, finely chopped
3-4 cloves garlic, finely chopped
1 onion, sliced
1 tbsp whole spices (peppercorns, cinnamon and clove)
1 tbsp mint leaves, finely chopped
1 tbsp coriander leaves, chopped
3-4 green chilies, slit

METHOD

Heat ghee in a skillet. Add the whole spices and bay leaf. Once it crackles, add the onion and sauté for a minute.

Add ginger and garlic and sauté for a minute.

Add the rice and fry for another minute.

Add salt and 2 cups of water. Bring it to a boil.

Reduce the heat, cover with a lid and cook for 10-15 minutes till the rice is done.

Reduce the heat and mix in the broccoli florets and cover again.

Switch off the flame and cook for 5-7 minutes in steam.

Serve hot with pomegranate raita.

CREAM OF BROCCOLI

INGREDIENTS

1 tbsp olive oil
1 tsp minced garlic
Salt and pepper to taste
200 g broccoli florets, blanched
1 cup cream
1 cup milk
1 tsp white pepper
1 tsp lemon juice
1 tbsp parmesan cheese

METHOD

In a skillet, add garlic and sauté for a minute.

Puree broccoli in a blender, add milk and blend until smooth.

Sieve and add to the skillet along with 1 cup of water.

Cover and cook for 10 minutes on low flame, stirring occasionally.

Add salt and pepper.

Add cream and lemon juice.

Sprinkle with parmesan cheese and serve.

BROCCOLI AND CHEESE CUTLETS

INGREDIENTS

150 g broccoli florets, blanched
150 g potatoes, boiled and mashed
Salt and pepper to taste
30 g processed cheese, grated
1 cup cornflour
1 cup breadcrumbs
2 tbsp olive oil

METHOD

In a bowl, add broccoli, potatoes, salt, pepper and cheese and mix well.

Check seasoning and make equal sized cutlets from the mixture.

Now mix cornflour and 3 tbsp of water and make a slurry.

Dip each cutlet in the slurry and coat lightly with breadcrumbs.

Preheat oven to 200°C.

Brush cutlets with a little olive oil and bake in the oven for 10 minutes or until light golden in colour.

Serve hot with your favourite sauce.

VEGETABLE SOUP

INGREDIENTS

1 tsp olive oil
½ tsp minced garlic
2-3 carrot slices
1 tbsp spring onions, sliced
2-3 broccoli florets
2 cups vegetable broth

METHOD

Heat a saucepan, sauté garlic until translucent.

Add all the vegetables and sauté for 1-2 minutes.

Now add the vegetable broth, salt and pepper and cook for 3-4 minutes.

Serve hot.

Food for Thought:

Some of you are aware of this superfood but do not know how to include it in your diet. Nutritionists say that to get the best benefits of broccoli, you should eat it raw or with minimum cooking. In fact, broccoli tastes best when it is cooked less to retain the crunch of the vegetable. Steaming, stir-fry or microwaving are the best options. Broccoli is very versatile and can be used in salads, soups, side dishes and in main courses. There are numerous options for you to choose from depending on your taste—from broccoli salad, steamed broccoli to broccoli pulao and broccoli paratha. There's even the kids' favourite broccoli bajji recipe. Here, I have a collection of Indian style broccoli recipes, both North Indian and South Indian, Chinese style broccoli recipes and many other international broccoli recipes. Try these simple recipes and enjoy the health benefits of broccoli!

CELERY

Minding Your Migraine

Celery is a plant that is consumed as a vegetable and is found all over the world. The taste is incredible and this vegetable is an important ingredient in soups, broths and salads! Celery is the most important part of different cultures' cuisines. The benefit of having celery is that it helps to lower cholesterol level. It takes away arthritis pain and also helps to lose weight quickly. It is rich in vitamin C and hence proves extremely beneficial for your health.

Celery is used in soups and salads as garnish. It is also eaten as a snack.

Celery comes with high nutritional value like sodium, copper, iron, zinc, potassium and calcium. It also contains fatty acids and vitamins A, C, E, D, B-6, B-12 and K. It also contains riboflavin, thiamin, fibre and folic acid.

Here are some health benefits that can be achieved

from consumption of celery.

Celery helps to reduce blood pressure. It contains a natural chemical compound that helps to lower stress hormones in blood. This is said to help the blood vessels to expand, allowing your blood more room to move, which eventually reduces pressure. Reduced blood pressure puts less stress on the entire cardiovascular system. This reduces chances of heart attacks.

Eating celery daily reduces cholesterol and therefore it is recommended to have this vegetable on the plate.

The seeds of celery help to eliminate uric acid as it stimulates urination. Therefore, celery is good for people who are suffering from bladder disorders, cystitis and kidney problems. The seeds also help in preventing urinary tract infections in women.

Celery is sodium and potassium rich and these minerals help to balance the fluid in the body. Potassium also helps in reducing blood pressure.

This incredible vegetable gives you relief from migraines.

It also treats muscular pains and arthritis. Celery leaves help in the treatment of diabetes as they are high in fibre. Celery tea drops can help to treat and improve your eyesight. Due to the presence of high calcium in this plant, celery helps to calm nerves.

This amazing vegetable has high levels of antioxidants and acts as a natural anti-inflammatory. It reduces symptoms related to inflammation, like joint pain and irritable bowel syndrome. Celery juice is also beneficial for your health. Weight loss, improvement in digestion and enhanced immune system are the few benefits which one can get from celery juice. It greatly helps to purify the blood. And most importantly, fresh celery juice helps to curb the craving for sweets.

Celery is mostly used for dressing but I have worked upon recipes that will prove to be complete sources of energy.

CELERY JUICE

INGREDIENTS

1 celery stalk, chopped
1 tbsp sugar syrup
1 tsp lemon juice
1 lemon, cut into wedges
A pinch of black salt

METHOD

In a mortar and pestle, muddle celery and lemon wedges.

Transfer to a cocktail mixer and add sugar syrup, lemon juice and black salt. Shake well.

Sieve and serve chilled.

CELERY SALAD

INGREDIENTS

3 tbsp olive oil
1 fresh Thai red chilli, chopped
2 celery stalks, thinly sliced
1/3 cup walnuts, toasted
2 tbsp fresh lime juice
Salt and pepper to taste
1 cucumber, roughly chopped

METHOD

In a bowl, mix oil, lime juice, salt and pepper.

Add the rest of the ingredients and toss.

Serve.

CELERY SOUP

INGREDIENTS

1 celery, stalks chopped
1 potato, chopped
1 onion, chopped
1 tbsp butter
Salt and pepper to taste
1 tbsp fresh dill
½ cup cream

METHOD

In a skillet, melt butter and then add onions, celery, potato and sauté for 2-3 minutes.

Add 2 cups of water, salt, pepper and cook further for 10-15 minutes or until potatoes are soft and mushy. Let it cool.

Now add dill and then transfer to a blender.

Puree and strain.

Now add cream and stir until well-combined.

Serve hot.

CELERY AND ORANGE SALAD

INGREDIENTS

2 celery stalks, very thinly sliced
1 tbsp fresh flat-leaf parsley with tender stems
3 tbsp fresh lemon juice
3 tbsp olive oil
¼ cup raisins
Salt and pepper to taste
2 ounces parmesan, shaved
Pulp of 1 orange, skin removed

METHOD

In a bowl, add lemon juice, olive oil, celery, parsley, raisins, salt, pepper and orange. Toss until well-combined. Garnish with fresh parmesan and serve.

FISH WITH CELERY AND CAPERS

INGREDIENTS

350 g fish
Salt and pepper to taste
1 tbsp lemon juice
2 large celery stalks with leaves, thinly sliced
2 tbsp capers

METHOD

In a bowl, marinate fish with salt, pepper and lemon juice for 10 minutes.

Heat a griddle pan. Add olive oil and grill fish until cooked, for approximately 2-3 minutes.

Add celery and capers in the fish marinade and give it a quick toss. Season with salt and pepper.

Serve with grilled fish.

Food for Thought:
Though this vegetable isn't very popular in India, yet I recommend it to be used in our daily diet because of its benefits.

A simple vegetable broth with celery will increase the nutritional food value of the broth. It can be used in gravies, sauces and even in pastas. So what are you waiting for? Go to your closest vegetable market and get this amazing vegetable home today and prepare something interesting with it for your family and friends.

If you are not very fond of cooking, you can simply serve celery as part of the finger salad in your party with some interesting dips!

GREEN LEAFY VEGETABLES

Red Lighting Mental Deterioration

We keep hearing from everyone that one must have green vegetables. But the question is: why? And here is the answer. Green leafy vegetables are extremely important to maintain your health since they are loaded with vitamins A and K which help fight inflammation and keep bones strong. It is necessary to have greens on your plate for every meal of the day. A diet filled with leafy vegetables protects us from various diseases and heart-related problems.

Green vegetables are high in fibre and low in fat and calories. This helps to maintain your weight by controlling your hunger. Being rich in magnesium, dietary fibre, vitamin C, potassium and folic acid, green vegetables are extremely good for your health. Presence of phytochemicals in them adds a healthy icing on your cake.

As they are rich in magnesium and have low glycemic index, they are good for diabetic patients as well.

Being rich in vitamin C, leafy vegetables easily produce an important protein for bone health called osteocalcin that keeps your bones stronger. Leafy vegetables like spinach and broccoli are main sources of iron and calcium.

These vegetables keep your eyesight healthy and prevent the risk of eye diseases.

Green leafy vegetables contain a lot of water that helps you to remain hydrated, thereby making your skin glow and look beautiful. Being a complete source of nutrition, the green vegetables also help in repairing and growing your body tissues. You might go green with fury or envy, but our humble green vegetables help to improve your mood, keeping you calm and healthy.

Normally, leafy vegetables are easy to cook and are easily available as well. Most of the leafy vegetables are seasonal, hence it is recommended to have them in their particular season. Just a word of caution: they are to be avoided in the rainy season as there are more chances of worms to be found in them.

You can have them in any form—boiled, sautéed, cooked, steamed and as soups and salads.

Not all are fond of green vegetables, especially kids. However, it is recommended to include them in every meal. Most of the kids get a little cranky when they see a lot of greens on their plates, but at the same time it is crucial to give them these greens as they are high in nutrition. An interesting fact about greens is that you can camouflage them very easily and make exciting recipes that would be happily enjoyed by your children.

I have worked on recipes that are exciting yet have medicinal values. At the same time, they are quick to prepare and easy to serve!

GREENS SALAD

INGREDIENTS

1 bowl fresh greens (baby spinach, arugula, rocket leaves)
¼ cup onion, chopped
1 tbsp garlic, minced
¼ tsp red pepper flakes, crushed
3 tbsp apple cider vinegar
Salt to taste

METHOD

In a bowl, mix all the ingredients and toss well until well-combined.

GRILLED TRUFFLE ASPARAGUS

INGREDIENTS

300 g asparagus, blanched
Salt and pepper to taste
1 tbsp truffle oil
1 tsp olive oil

METHOD

Heat a griddle pan and sauté the blanched asparagus for 2-3 minutes.
Season with salt and pepper.
Drizzle truffle oil on top and serve.

SAUTÉED GARLIC SPINACH

INGREDIENTS

1 tsp olive oil
Salt and pepper to taste
150 g spinach
1 tsp garlic, minced

METHOD

Heat olive oil in a pan.
Add garlic and sauté for a minute.
Now add spinach and season with salt and pepper.
Cook for 2-3 minutes or until it changes colour.
Serve it as a side with fish or chicken, or enjoy it as it is.

GREENS PULAO WITH CHICKPEAS

INGREDIENTS

1 cup basmati rice, washed and soaked (for 30 minutes in water)
1 cup spinach, washed and leaves chopped (discard stems)
¼ cup fenugreek greens, washed and leaves chopped (discard stems)
1 onion, thinly sliced
2-3 green chillies, finely chopped
½ tsp cumin seeds
½ tsp asafoetida powder
1" ginger, finely chopped
1 tbsp ghee
½ tsp garam masala
1 cup boiled chickpeas
1 tsp red chilli powder

METHOD

Heat ½ tbsp of ghee in a pressure cooker.

Add asafoetida. Once it crackles, add cumin seeds. Let it crackle and then add onions and sauté until light golden in colour.

Now add rice and sauté for 1 minute on high flame.

Add 1 ½ cups of water, add salt and garam masala. Cook under pressure for 10 minutes and then let it cook in steam.

In another pan, heat ½ tbsp ghee, add ginger and sauté for a minute, then add spinach, fenugreek leaves, salt, chilli powder and chickpeas. Cook for 10 minutes on low flame.

After the rice cools, layer it alternately with the greens and chickpeas.

Cover with foil and bake in an oven preheated to 200°C for 10 minutes.

Serve hot with curd.

FENUGREEK MULTIGRAIN ROTI

INGREDIENTS

3 cups fenugreek leaves, finely chopped
1 cup multigrain atta
½ besan or chickpea flour
3-4 green chillies, finely chopped
1 onion, finely chopped
½ tsp red chilli powder
Salt to taste
Water as required
1 tbsp olive oil

METHOD

In a bowl, add the chopped fenugreek, atta, besan, salt, chilli powder and onion, and knead a dough.

Divide the dough into equal portions and make balls of each portion.

Flatten each ball into a roti and cook both sides on a hot tawa till it's fully cooked (till you see brown spots on the roti).

Then brush lightly with olive oil and cook for ½ a minute or until light golden and crisp.

Enjoy!

Food for Thought:
A healthy food habit is the future trend and green leafy vegetable is leading the march here. I see people all over the world getting into good eating habits. People are looking at recipes which are delicious and healthy at the same time, and that is what my idea as a chef is—to not just make such recipes but have those recipes reach out to as many people so that we all can have a healthy and happy life!

I remember my grandmother telling me that there is nothing more in life than good health. You can enjoy every pleasure of life if you are healthy, and if you aren't, everything is tasteless and flavourless. Now I realize the wisdom in her words. Health is our true wealth!

WALNUTS

Going `Nuts'? Have Walnuts

Walnuts are edible seeds that come from trees. They are round and are single-seeded fruits of the walnut tree. I'm sure most of you have seen the fruit and the seed of walnut which is inside a thick husk. The seeds contain some important nutrients, such as vitamins, proteins, carbohydrates and minerals. The shell is also used in beauty products, especially in making body scrubs, etc.

It is interesting that the structure of walnuts has a crinkly appearance just like the brain. According to scientific studies, eating walnuts helps in optimum functioning of the brain since they contain omega fatty acids.

Apart from the delicious taste, walnuts have proteins and antioxidants that help in improving health. They are delicious and can be easily included in the diet. They are also considered to be 'power food' as they help to build and improve stamina.

Below are some interesting facts about walnuts:

Walnuts have been known to human beings from 7000 B.C. Apart from protecting the heart, reducing the risk of cancer and promoting hair growth, it also benefits the skin in many ways. If your skin is uneven and dull, and your enlarged pores make you look old and unhealthy, eating walnuts everyday will help to tighten your pores and improve your skin texture.

In today's times, pollution, unhygienic environment and junk food give you serious pimple problems and sometimes pimples are stubborn and unpleasant to look at. In order to get rid of them, a handful of walnuts is a perfect solution. Having walnuts can make your skin super shiny and glowing, and after all, who doesn't like a clear and beautiful skin!

Hectic schedules are a way of life nowadays which means not enough sleep, which of course makes you age faster. Getting fine wrinkles at an early age is no happiness and this is why eating walnuts helps a lot. It will not only make your skin glow but will also boost your mood that will lower your stress and keep you energetic throughout the day.

Dark circles are a major concern for everyone. Incorporating walnuts in your daily food will help you get rid of dark circles and the puffiness around your eyes. You can find your eyes healthy and beautiful. Walnuts are superfoods and I recommend it to be included in your daily diet.

Here are some quick ideas how you can include walnuts in your daily diet:

You can crush them and sprinkle as garnish on a dish.

You can simply pop them up on a dish and garnish them.

You can also use them in salads and milkshakes.

Walnuts can improve your cognitive health. Their high levels of antioxidants, vitamins and minerals also improve mental alertness. The vitamin E in the nuts can also ward off Alzheimer's. I have come up with recipes with walnuts that are delicious and interesting.

MEDITERRANEAN SALAD WITH ROASTED WALNUTS

INGREDIENTS

1 cup cucumber, chopped
1 tomato, roughly chopped
1 onion, roughly chopped
½ cup yellow pepper, roughly chopped
½ cup red pepper, roughly chopped
¼ cup green capsicum, roughly chopped
4-5 mint leaves, crushed with hands
1 tbsp lemon juice
2 tbsp olive oil
Salt and pepper to taste
½ cup feta cheese, crumbled
1 cup walnuts, roasted

METHOD

In a bowl, mix all the vegetables.

In another bowl, mix lemon juice, salt, pepper and olive oil. Whisk until all the ingredients are well-combined.

Drizzle on top of the mixed salad and toss until well-combined.

Sprinkle feta cheese and walnuts on the salad and serve.

WALNUT CEREAL HEALTH BARS

INGREDIENTS

1 cup oats, toasted on a non-stick pan
1 cup chopped walnuts, crushed
3 cups puffed rice
2 tbsp honey
1 cup jaggery, melted

METHOD

In a non-stick pan, toast oats for a minute and let them cool on a plate.

Now in the same pan, toast the puffed rice for 2-3 minutes or until lightly toasted.

Now roast walnuts in the same pan for 1 minute or so and keep it aside to cool at room temperature.

In a bowl, combine all the above ingredients.

Melt jaggery in a pan on medium heat, stirring continuously, making sure it does not get burnt (approx 2-3 minutes).

Add honey and the mixed ingredients and mix well until well-combined.

Grease a rectangular dish with olive oil and transfer the prepared mixture into it, pressing down the sides, spreading evenly.

Now with the help of a knife, cut it into rectangular bars before it cools.

Once it cools, take the bars out of the dish and keep them in an airtight container.

PEAS AND WALNUT SOUP

INGREDIENTS

1 cup walnuts, lightly crushed
1 cup boiled and pureed peas
1 cup milk
1 tsp white pepper
½ cup cream
1 cup vegetable stock
1 tbsp cornflour
Salt to taste

METHOD

In a pan, roast walnuts for 1 minute, then take them off flame and keep them aside to cool.

In another pan, heat vegetable stock, milk and cream. Add salt and pepper.

Sieve the peas puree and add it to the above.

Mix cornflour in 1 tbsp water and add to the above.

Boil it and let it thicken.

Add walnuts and serve hot.

WALNUTS AND BEANS

INGREDIENTS

200 g French beans, washed and trimmed
1 tsp olive oil
Salt and pepper to taste
½ cup walnuts, toasted

METHOD

In a saucepan, boil water and blanch the beans. Drain and keep in cold water for 5 minutes, then drain.

In a pan, heat oil, add French beans and sauté for a minute. Then season with salt and pepper.

Sprinkle toasted walnuts.

Serve and enjoy!

BULGUR AND WALNUTS PULAO

INGREDIENTS

2 tbsp extra-virgin olive oil
1 onion, chopped
1 tbsp garlic, finely chopped
1½ cups bulgur, preferably medium or coarse
½ tsp saffron, soaked in 1 tsp milk
½ tsp ground cumin
2 cups vegetable broth, or reduced-sodium chicken broth
1 tsp salt
¼ cup fresh mint, chopped
½ cup walnuts, toasted and chopped

METHOD

In a skillet, heat oil, add onion and cook, stirring for 1-2 minutes until golden brown.

Add garlic and sauté for 1 minute. Add bulgur, cumin and saffron. Cook for about 1 minute, stirring continuously.

Add broth and salt and bring to a boil. Cover and cook on medium flame, for approximately 15 minutes, until bulgur is cooked. Remove from the heat and keep it covered for 5 minutes until the steam settles.

Stir in mint and garnish with walnuts, and serve.

HAREES WITH WALNUTS

INGREDIENTS

1 cup rice
1 cup chicken, boneless and shredded
1 tbsp ghee
1 onion, chopped
Salt to taste
1 cup walnuts, finely chopped
½ tsp black pepper
1 tsp cumin seeds
½ cup walnuts, crushed

METHOD

In a skillet, heat ghee, add cumin seeds, add onions and sauté until translucent.

Add rice, chicken, salt and pepper. Cover and cook, stirring frequently.

Cover and cook again for 40-45 minutes, mashing the chicken with the ladle as you stir, so that it is fully mixed with the rice.

Top it with walnuts and serve hot!

Food for Thought:
You will always find a packet of walnuts in my handbag when I travel as it keeps me away from nibbling on junk or anything that is unhealthy, and also suffices my hunger pangs. It is the best way to keep yourself healthy even while travelling and is easily available in stores. Winters in Shimla are so cold! I remember those times when my grandmother and mother used to prepare walnut and jaggery bites, flavoured with fennel seeds—they were by far the best dessert for winters! It was in a brick form and used to be served in winters. It was really a delight to have it made by combining jaggery, clarified butter, roasted fennel seeds and roasted walnuts, all cooked together for a while but not caramelized, and then poured over a greased tray, unmoulded when cold, cut into square pieces and kept in a container. Simply yummy! My grandmother used to tell me, 'Eat it beta as it will keep you warm but have it in moderation.' But being as naughty as I was, and with a big sweet tooth, I would gobble it up like there was no tomorrow. Little did I understand then what she was trying to say, but now I do, hence sharing the knowledge with you.

Walnuts, I guess, also give you wisdom!

ROSEMARY

'Nerves' of Steel

Rosemary is native to the Mediterranean region. In the ancient times, Greeks believed it to be a magical plant that helped in strengthening memory. And you will not doubt that, considering the immense contribution of Greeks in thoughts and theories and their art of rhetoric. This almost-magical plant is also used as a herbal medicine for relief from toothache, gas, headache and baldness. Rosemary goes extremely well with meats. It comes with a great taste and strong aroma, and benefits health if incorporated in your diet. It belongs to the family of mint but has a distinctive flavour. It has a kind of warm taste that can be used in flavouring sauces, stews, soups, etc. It is extensively used in Italian cuisine and in the year 2000, rosemary was named as Herb of the Year by the International Herb Association.

Normally, herbs that give flavour to food are not considered to have a large impact on your health, but when it comes to rosemary, it is a different story altogether. Rosemary is not only used in food but it is also used in oil, tea and other products. In fact, you can directly rub rosemary on your skin. You can also grow rosemary in your garden but with one precaution: rosemary is not a water-friendly plant so avoid overusing water. I have a few herbs in my kitchen garden and in fact, one has grown up to five feet. If the herb is well-preserved and dried, it can give a fantastic flavour to your food.

Apart from this, rosemary comes with many medicinal benefits. It is a great source of vitamins, calcium and iron. It eases muscle pain and also greatly helps to improve memory. It helps to boost your immune and circulatory systems as well.

Rosemary is an interesting ingredient when it comes to recipes. It is not at all easy to make a recipe that is also helpful medicinally. Yet, through a lot of research I have come up with interesting recipes that will spice up your mood and at the same time work greatly on your health. Carnosic acid, one of the main components of rosemary, helps to protect the brain from neuro-degeneration. It protects the brain from chemical-free radicals which cause Alzheimer's, strokes and normal ageing.

Though it isn't an Indian herb, yet due to its benefits I recommend it to be put in your diet, especially in winters. It also goes very well with pastas and meats. Since it has such an amazing taste, this herb surely cannot be ignored!

ROSEMARY SCONES

INGREDIENTS

1 ½ cups butter
1 tbsp fresh rosemary, chopped
2 ¾ cups all-purpose flour
¼ tsp salt

METHOD

In a medium bowl, cream the butter until light and fluffy. Stir in the flour, salt and rosemary until well-blended. The dough will be somewhat soft. Cover and refrigerate for 1 hour.

Preheat the oven to 180°C. Place parchment paper on the baking tray.

On a lightly floured surface, roll out the dough to ¼" thickness. Cut into rectangles, 1 ½x2" in size. Place scones 2" apart on the lined baking tray.

Bake for 8 minutes in the preheated oven, or until golden at the edges. Cool on wire racks and store in an airtight container at room temperature.

SMOKED APPLE AND ROSEMARY SOUP

INGREDIENTS

2 apples, boiled (until soft)
Salt and pepper to taste
1 tsp lemon juice
1 sprig fresh rosemary

METHOD

Peel apples and de-seed.
Puree in a blender until smooth.
Add chilled milk, salt and pepper.
Smoke rosemary on open fire and add to the above mixture.
Sieve and serve chilled in glasses.

GARLIC AND ROSEMARY MUSHROOMS

INGREDIENTS

300 g mushrooms
2 cloves garlic, finely chopped
½ cup onions, finely chopped
1½ tsp fresh rosemary, chopped
¼ tsp salt and pepper to taste
1 tbsp olive oil

METHOD

Heat the oil in a skillet over medium heat.

Add garlic and sauté for a minute.

Then add onions and cook until translucent.

Now add mushrooms, rosemary, salt and pepper, and cook, stirring occasionally for approximately 10 minutes.

Pour in a dash of water and cook for 30 seconds to 1 minute.

POTATO WEDGES

INGREDIENTS

2 medium-sized sweet potatoes, cut into wedges
1 tbsp olive oil
½ tsp salt
¼ tsp black pepper
1 tbsp fresh rosemary

METHOD

In a bowl, mix all the ingredients and toss well.

Preheat oven to 180°C.

Transfer into a baking tray and bake for 30-40 minutes or until soft from inside and crisp from outside.

ROASTED ROSEMARY CHICKEN

INGREDIENTS

1 kg boneless chicken breasts
1-2 lemons, cut into wedges
2 sprigs rosemary
2 garlic cloves, crushed
1 tbsp extra virgin olive oil
1 tsp salt
½ tsp black pepper
1 tsp cayenne pepper

METHOD

Preheat oven to 200°C.

Layer the baking dish with potatoes, 1 sprig of rosemary and crushed garlic, and mix.

Rub the chicken with salt, pepper and olive oil and lay it on top.

Bake for 40-60 minutes until chicken is cooked. Cover with aluminum foil and let it rest for 5-10 minutes.

Serve with lemon wedges and a sprig of rosemary.

Food for Thought:
I love smoking rosemary before adding it to my dishes. It simply gives an extra flavour and the aroma is outstanding as its oil is secreted. I love to add it to cocktails as well as to roasts. For me, it is a winter herb, simply because it is strong and goes very well with meats, and winter is a time in India where one can really indulge in elaborate meals and heavy food.

Rosemary scones are my favourites with tea. I once had a Sunday roast which was made with rosemary, and it was simply awesome. That's when I fell in love at first bite with rosemary!

ALMONDS

Fasten Your Seat Belts, Brain on Full Throttle

And now make way for almonds! Being the most popular nut worldwide and a source of many nutrients which help in the development and health of the human brain, almonds have always been associated with higher intellect. They have long been considered an essential food item for the growing children. They also contain two vital nutrients which have shown to increase brain activity, resulting in new neural pathways and a decreased occurrence of Alzheimer's disease. Studies have shown that almonds in the diet, as well as almond oil, are beneficial to our overall health and the functioning of the nervous system.

Two or three pieces of soaked almonds are enough, and you can also remove the outer shell if it causes allergic reactions, as majority of the nutrients are not held in the shell. I have been fed soaked almonds and honey all through my childhood by my grandmother. I recommend it to be included in your daily diet too. They are the healthiest among all the tree nuts available and are full of minerals. Almonds are a rich source of calcium, vitamin E, potassium, proteins, fibre and magnesium. And the sugar content is low.

Eating almonds will help you have a healthy heart as it is a good source of magnesium which prevents the risk of strokes and hypertension.

Since ancient times it has been considered the best food for the brain. In my home, it is a ritual to have overnight soaked almonds with honey along with breakfast. The presence of vitamin E and antioxidants help to nourish your skin and make it healthy. Also the presence of antioxidants helps to fight skin cancer.

Almonds contain monounsaturated fatty acids which slow down the release of glucose into the bloodstream and help in fighting diabetes. Being rich in dietary fibres and healthy fats, almonds are highly beneficial for weight loss. The fibre helps the stomach to remain full for long hours. Also, they help in lowering bad cholesterol which eventually helps in weight loss. An important function of almonds is that they help to maintain alkaline balance of the body and make bones and teeth strong.

I can eat almonds anytime, anywhere and I do carry in my handbag a box of almonds, walnuts and raisins to suffice my hunger pangs. While travelling, it helps me avoid eating unhealthy food. It is a magical nut that keeps me energetic and going throughout the day.

Almonds benefit the skin by making it healthy and glowing. There are different types of available products made from almonds that help greatly in the treatment of your skin. Almond milk and almond oil help to nourish the skin and make it glow.

Almond is truly a global nut and one can find a lot of its usage throughout the world. Here are a few of my favourite recipes which I am sharing with you. Hope you find them interesting and fun to cook!

FISH WITH ALMOND CRUST

INGREDIENTS

¼ cup almond powder
1 tbsp dry breadcrumbs
1 tsp garlic, finely chopped
½ tsp black pepper
1 tbsp olive oil
2 salmon fillets
1 tbsp lemon juice
fresh parsley, chopped
1 tbsp parmesan cheese, grated
1 lemon, cut into wedges

METHOD

In a bowl, mix almond powder, breadcrumbs salt, pepper, cheese and parsley.

Marinate fish with lemon juice, garlic and salt for 10 minutes.

Heat oil in a large non-stick pan. Now coat each fillet lightly with the prepared almond mixture.

Cook for 3 minutes on each side or until fish flakes.

Serve with lemon wedges.

BOTTLE UP THE ALMONDS

INGREDIENTS

1 tbsp olive oil
2 cups almonds
¼ tsp cayenne pepper
1 tsp paprika
¾ tsp salt

METHOD

Preheat the oven to 180°C and line a baking tray with parchment paper. Grease evenly with a little olive oil.

Bake the almonds for 20 minutes in the oven. Then take them out of the oven and let them cool.

In a large bowl, mix salt, paprika and cayenne pepper until well-combined and toss the almonds in the mixture until evenly coated.

It can be bottled up and kept in an airtight container and enjoyed!

WASABI ALMONDS

INGREDIENTS

500 g prawns
1 cup sliced almonds, lightly toasted
½ tsp salt
½ tsp freshly ground black pepper
1 cup mayonnaise
½ tsp wasabi paste

METHOD

In a pan, heat oil and sauté the prawns for 2-3 minutes or until cooked (make sure not to overcook as it will become very chewy).

Season with salt and pepper and mix well. Take it off flame.

Now in a bowl, mix mayonnaise, wasabi and salt until well-combined.

Now toss the prawns in this mixture and coat each prawn individually with the sliced almonds.

Serve immediately!

ALMOND BUTTER COOKIES

INGREDIENTS

¼ cup flour
1 cup wholewheat flour
1 tsp baking soda
¼ cup butter at room temperature
¾ cup almond butter
²/₃ cup brown sugar
½ tsp vanilla extract
1 egg
¼ cup almonds, cut into halves

METHOD

Preheat the oven to 190°C. Cover the baking tray with parchment paper.

In a bowl, whisk the flours, salt and baking soda together.

In another bowl, cream the butter, almond butter and sugar until fluffy.

Now add vanilla extract and egg, and mix until well-combined. Gradually, stir the flour mixture, blending well.

Shape the dough into ¼" equal sized balls, flatten on top and place them on the baking sheets.

Place an almond half in the centre of each flattened ball.

Bake for 12-13 minutes, until lightly golden.

Cool at room temperature and store in an airtight container.

NOODLES WITH ALMOND SAUCE

INGREDIENTS

¼ cup sliced almonds, lightly toasted
¾ lb whole wheat noodles
1 tsp garlic, minced
Salt and pepper to taste
4-5 broccoli florets
2 cups snow peas, trimmed
¼ cup capsicum juliennes
1 tbsp soy sauce
3 tbsp fresh lime juice
1 tbsp chilli sauce
½ cup green onions, thinly sliced

METHOD

Bring a large pot of water to a boil and cook the noodles for approximately 10-12 minutes.

Sieve and run the noodles under cold water and save the boiled water.

Add the broccoli to the boiled water and keep for 1 minute and then add the snow peas and keep for a minute. Drain and keep the vegetables aside.

In a pan, heat oil, add garlic and sauté until translucent. Now add spring onions and sauté for half a minute. Then add soy sauce, lime juice, chilli sauce and the vegetables. Cook for a minute on high flame, stirring continuously.

Now add the noodles and lightly toss them with the help of chopsticks or a fork.

Season with salt and pepper according to taste.

Serve garnished with toasted almonds.

ALMOND TARTS

INGREDIENTS

½ cup almond flour
½ cup flour
¼ cup oats
¼ cup brown sugar
¼ cup toasted almonds
½ tsp cinnamon powder
½ cup chilled butter
¼ cup sugar
2 tbsp lemon juice
2 eggs, whisked
2 egg yolks, whisked

METHOD

In a bowl, add flour, almond flour, oats and brown sugar, and mix well.

Now add in butter and mix until mixture is crumbly and resembles breadcrumbs. Make a dough and refrigerate (add water if required) for 30 minutes.

Preheat oven to 180°C.

Roll the dough lightly with a rolling pin. Cover the base of a tart mould with the dough, pressing with your fingers. Spread it evenly at the base and the edges.

Prick with a fork and cover with foil and bake for 10 minutes. This is called blind baking!

Once baked, allow it to cool at room temperature.

Now in another bowl, mix sugar mixture, toasted almonds, lemon juice and eggs.

Transfer the mixture into the baked tart shell and bake again for 30-40 minutes until golden and wobbly in the centre.

Take it out of the oven and let it cool at room temperature.

Slice and serve!

Food for Thought:
Among the many family recipes that I've shared with you, one of them is 'hot almond milk' which is a ritual in my house in Shimla during winters.
My grandmother and mother used to prepare almond milk by sautéing almonds in a little clarified butter and then adding it to hot milk along with saffron and honey.
It is very comforting in winters and keeps one warm as well!
Try this recipe;
I'm sure you will enjoy it too.

EGG YOLK

Eggs are Forever

Boil them, scramble them, poach them or fry them. Eggs will be there for you, forever. Egg yolks contain a large amount of choline, which helps in foetal brain development. It also breaks down a chemical that produces hormones related to happiness. And yes, it is also one of the most inexpensive sources of protein out in the market.

Eggs fall into one of those rare categories of food which in itself is a complete meal. Chicken eggs are most popular and are easily available, and there are numerous recipes that can be prepared with them. Eggs can be eaten for any meal—breakfast, lunch, evening snack or dinner. Even for that late-night binging.

Eggs come with a high nutrient value and therefore you will see athletes and health conscious people consuming it daily. It helps in muscle building and maintaining and improving your health. Egg is one of the ingredients which can be eaten uncooked or cooked. Uncooked egg mixed in milk is very good for undernourished or underweight people.

Eggs come with high quality protein and also have important vitamins and minerals, which play a very important role in one's diet. It is a fascinating food and is loved by many, including me. One thing that you would find in my refrigerator at all times is eggs. Having six to eight eggs a week helps to balance your metabolism and maintain a balanced diet.

Eggs are a rich source of antioxidants which are good for the eyes, and helps prevent harmful diseases and infections. It also lowers the chances of age-related diseases. These antioxidants are particularly in the yolk, which is why people are advised not to leave the yolk out. It is rich in vitamin A and the deficiency of which is a major cause of blindness.

Egg yolks are also full of many good-for-you nutrients, such as riboflavin, vitamin D and vitamin B-12. Plus, the yolk contains nutrients such as choline and selenium and omega 3 fats as well. It helps to decrease blood pressure and improve the vascular functioning of the body.

And who doesn't know the conditioning quality of egg when it is applied to your hair! It makes the hair look shinier and removes frizziness. And exactly how does it do that? Well, the yolk of egg moisturizes the scalp and removes dryness.

Not everyone likes to eat eggs and many people avoid tasting the egg yolk. The yolk too can be used in various interesting recipes. Here are some recipes which are quick to make and very healthy.

HOLLANDAISE

INGREDIENTS

2 egg yolks
100 g butter, melted
1 tsp lemon juice or vinegar
Salt to taste
½ tsp mustard powder

METHOD

Whisk egg yolks, salt, lemon juice and mustard.

While whisking, slowly keep adding butter. Whisk continuously till well-incorporated.

If you feel it is about to split then add an ice cube and whisk again.

MAYONNAISE

INGREDIENTS

1 egg yolk
1 cup oil
1 tsp mustard powder
1 tbsp lemon juice
Salt
A pinch of sugar (optional)

METHOD

Whisk eggs, salt, sugar, lemon juice and mustard powder together in a bowl.

While whisking, start adding oil, a little at a time.

Continue until the mixture begins to thicken and becomes lighter in colour.

This is the sign that the emulsion has formed. At this point, you can start adding the oil in a thin stream till fully incorporated.

Bottle it up and then refrigerate. It stays fresh for a week.

CRÈME BRÛLÉE

INGREDIENTS

300 ml heavy cream
500 ml milk
4 egg yolks
220 g caster sugar
1 tsp vanilla essence
A pinch of nutmeg
1 cup castor sugar for caramelization

METHOD

In a large saucepan, add cream and milk and bring to a boil. Then take it off flame.

Meanwhile, in another bowl, whisk the yolks, sugar, nutmeg and vanilla, and slowly pour the hot milk mix, whisking constantly.

Put it back in the pan and heat gently, stirring until the custard becomes thick and covers the back of a spoon.

Transfer into ramekins and chill in the refrigerator.

When cold, sprinkle some sugar and with the help of a blowtorch, caramelize it and serve!

COCONUT PUDDING

INGREDIENTS

1 cup coconut milk
1 cup cream
¾ cup sugar
2 egg yolks
½ cup coconut flakes

METHOD

In a saucepan, add coconut milk, cream and sugar, and bring to a boil.

Stir in egg yolks and add a ladle of the cream mix in it. Stir and add it back to the saucepan.

Cook for 1 minute, stirring constantly with a whisk. Remove from heat and add coconut flakes to it.

Divide into ramekins and chill them in the refrigerator.

COOKIES

INGREDIENTS

- 1 cup butter
- 1½ cups sugar
- ½ tsp orange rind
- 3 eggs with yolks
- 2½ cups flour
- 1 tsp baking soda
- 1 tsp cream of tartar
- 1 tsp vanilla essence
- ½ tsp lemon juice

METHOD

Cream butter and sugar until fluffy.

Add eggs, orange rind, vanilla essence and lemon juice to the above and mix well.

In another bowl, mix flour, baking soda and cream of tartar and sieve.

Add the above dry ingredients to the egg mixture and mix until well-blended.

Preheat oven to 180°C for 10 minutes.

Now take an ice cream scooper and scoop out equal amounts of the mixture and put them on a baking tray lined with parchment paper.

Bake at 180°C for 10 minutes to make crisp cookies.

ORANGE CAKE

INGREDIENTS

1¾ cups flour
1½ tsp baking powder
2 egg yolks
1 egg
1 cup sugar
1 tbsp orange zest
½ cup orange juice, strained
¼ cup hot water

METHOD

Preheat oven to 180°C.

In a bowl, add flour, baking powder and salt, and sift together.

In a mixing bowl, beat egg yolks and eggs with an electric mixer for about 5 minutes.

Gradually add sugar, and once mixed, fold in orange zest and orange juice.

Fold in the flour alternately with hot water.

Pour batter into a greased baking dish.

Bake at 180°C for 45-50 minutes or till a toothpick inserted into the centre of the cake comes out clean.

Take it off the oven to cool at room temperature.

Once cool, dust with icing sugar and serve.

Food for Thought:
Egg yolks are great for health as they promote good cholesterol in the body. World Egg Day is celebrated every year on the second Friday of October, since the day was instituted in Vienna in 1996. It is held to celebrate and raise awareness of the benefits of eggs. But of course, with or without this day, your everyday can be the egg day, unless you have been medically advised against it. With only about 70 calories per large egg and lots of important nutrients, you should be eating the yolk too! The American Heart Association lists eggs as a 'Healthy Food for Under $1' making it a budget-friendly choice. Yolks have 40 per cent protein of the egg and it also has good cholesterol.

DARK CHOCOLATE

Liking the Heart, Loving the Brain

The moment we hear 'chocolate', most of us have a big ear-to-ear smile on our faces. Chocolate is happiness and this is why we exchange chocolates on happy occasions. And so, I am ending this book on a happy note with tantalizing recipes of dark chocolate.

Dark chocolate, also known as black chocolate or plain chocolate, is a form of chocolate which has a higher content of cocoa butter and less milk than other forms of chocolate. Dark chocolate contains antioxidants and has anti-inflammatory properties as well.

Chocolates have always been considered to give us calories, but wait, it isn't completely true. Different types of chocolates come with different health benefits. Dark chocolate is one of them and many people may not be aware that if eaten in the right quantity, dark chocolates will not beef you up with added calories.

Desserts are my weakness and I can't resist when offered a chocolate! It is true that dark chocolate is healthy as it comes with healthy compounds known as flavonoids, which are used in medicines. They help in treating ailments and offer various other health benefits.

When you enjoy a piece of dark chocolate, which is rich in cocoa, it will make you relaxed as it will release endorphins in the brain. This will help to enhance your mood and energy levels.

Dark chocolate contains flavonoids and antioxidants that help to increase the blood flow to the heart. Not just that, it also helps to bring down the blood pressure, thus putting off the risk of any heart attack.

Dark chocolate saves your skin from damages as it soaks up vitamin D from the sun. It helps to improve blood circulation, making your complexion better. It is hard to believe but it is true that cocoa can prevent your teeth from getting damaged as it acts as an antibacterial agent and prevents the growth of plague that causes bacteria on your teeth. I know I am breaking many myths here, but here is a simple, sweet fact: chocolates are known for their calories which means weight gain at every bite, but when it comes to dark chocolate, it is a different story altogether. The combination of bittersweet taste helps to control your appetite and makes your stomach feel full.

Normally, chocolates are avoided by diabetic patients. But dark chocolate is low in sugar content. In fact, the bitter taste will help you control the blood sugar level, but of course you should check with your doctor before consuming it.

Usually, many dessert recipes are prepared from dark chocolate but very few are aware that dark chocolate is also used medicinally. Here are some quick recipes made from dark chocolate which are not only delicious but extremely healthy too.

CHOCO POPS

INGREDIENTS

200 g dark chocolate
2 cups cream
¾ cup sugar
A pinch of salt
1 tsp vanilla

METHOD

In a saucepan, melt chocolate by double boiler method. Take it off flame.

In another bowl, whisk in cream, sugar, cocoa powder and salt together.

Now whisk sugar mixture into the chocolate mixture.

Cook and stir together until smooth.

Spoon the mixture into round moulds, thread them onto satay sticks and freeze for 5-6 hours until firm.

Unmould them and dip in melted dark chocolate.

Enjoy!

DARK CHOCOLATE CHIP COOKIES

Nothing beats a good old-fashioned dark chocolate recipe. Preparing dark chocolate chip cookies is a timeless classic and is worth to be called an iconic dessert.

INGREDIENTS

125 g dark chocolate
50 g cocoa powder
100 g flour
125 g brown sugar
1 tsp vanilla essence
1 egg
350 g dark choco chips
1 tsp soda
125 g butter at room temperature

METHOD

Preheat oven to 170°C and melt the dark chocolate by double boiler method.

In another bowl, mix the flour, cocoa and soda.

In another bowl, cream the butter and sugar, and add the melted chocolate and mix it well.

Beat the egg and vanilla essence and mix the dry ingredients by cut and fold method and stir in the chocolate chips.

Line a baking tray with parchment paper and with an ice cream scooper, scoop out equal proportions of the mixture on to it and lightly flatten each scoop.

Cook for 18-20 minutes until the sides look slightly golden in colour.

Take it off from the oven and let it cool at room temperature.

DARK CHOCOLATE ORANGE PUDDING

INGREDIENTS

10 slices of bread, sides removed
½ cup castor sugar
1 cup dark chocolate, melted
1 cup cream
½ cup butter
1 tsp vanilla extract
A pinch of cinnamon powder
1 tbsp orange rind
½ cup orange juice

METHOD

Preheat oven to 180°C.

In a bowl, mix orange juice, cream, sugar, cinnamon, melted chocolate, butter and orange rind.

Add the cream in a pan on flame and bring to a boil, stirring continuously for 2 minutes and add this to the above mixture.

Grease a baking dish with a little butter. Now arrange the slices of bread evenly.

Pour the chocolate mixture on top and bake for 20 minutes.

Serve hot.

DARK CHOCOLATE BISCUIT

INGREDIENTS

1 cup dark chocolate
$2/3$ cup castor sugar
2 whites of an egg (whisk till light and fluffy)
1 egg
1 tsp vanilla essence
$2/3$ cup milk
¾ cup walnuts

METHOD

Preheat oven to 180°C.

In a saucepan, mix milk, vanilla essence and egg and cook till thick. Let it cool.

In another bowl, mix melted chocolate and sugar and once the sugar melts, fold in the whisked egg whites.

Now combine both the mixtures lightly, making sure the air does not escape the mixture.

Transfer to greased ramekins and cook for 10 minutes.

Serve immediately!

CHICKEN WITH CHILLI CHOCOLATE SAUCE

INGREDIENTS

1 kg chicken
Juice of 2 lemons
(1 for the chicken and 1 for the sauce)
½ cup cocoa
1 tbsp flour
Salt and pepper to taste
2 tbsp oil
1 tbsp dark chocolate, melted
1 tsp honey
1 cup chicken broth
4-5 red chillies, finely chopped
1 tsp garlic, finely chopped
1 tbsp spring onions, thinly sliced

METHOD

Marinate chicken with salt, pepper and lemon juice for 30 minutes.

Heat a griddle pan till smoking hot.

Grease with oil and grill the chicken till cooked. Keep aside.

Simultaneously in a saucepan, heat oil. Sauté garlic for a minute and add spring onions and again sauté for 1 minute.

Add chillies, chicken broth and honey and reduce to half.

Add chocolate and chicken and cook till the consistency is saucy.

Serve hot.

CHOCOLATE MOUSSE

INGREDIENTS

1 cup dark chocolate, melted
½ cup powdered sugar
½ cup butter, softened
1¼ cup whipping cream
1 tbsp gelatine
½ cup cream cheese

METHOD

In a bowl, combine chocolate, sugar, butter and cream cheese and mix well.

In another bowl, whip the cream and add it to the above mixture and whisk together.

Now put gelatin in the microwave for 10 seconds. Once it dissolves whisk it with the cream and chocolate mixture.

Pour in glasses and chill in the refrigerator.

Garnish with chocolate shavings and cherry (optional).

Food for Thought:
Dark chocolate is one of the best known superfoods. It contains antioxidants and is considered healthier than any other type of chocolate. I love using it in my desserts, especially in chocolate cakes and brownies and you'll always find a box of chocolate brownies in my kitchen at any given time! So for those of you who like desserts and like to bake, you know what to shop for today!

THE CONCLUSION

I hope that with the turn of each new page of this recipe book, you have savoured the culinary journey with me. The importance of this book lies in the fact that food can also heal. Experimenting with ingredients to cook different dishes is quite enjoyable, but the real satisfaction lies in knowing that a lot of these ingredients can be beneficial to sharpen our mind, prevent disorders like ADHD, increase concentration and analytical abilities, fight stress and memory loss, etc. Some of these ingredients are even helpful in fighting more than one disorder. So one thing is for sure: never take cooking for granted as it has the magical power of healing.

And this magic is simple. Eating the right food gives energy to the body, which in turn helps the mind to communicate better with the body. When the mind transmits the right messages, all bodily functions are in harmony, and we achieve peace and tranquility within. We become one with ourself and our soul.

Hence the saintly saying goes, '*काहे रे वन खोजन जाओं सर्व निवासी सदा अलेप टोहि संग समाये रे वन खोजन जाओं।*' 'Why look outside when God resides within you?'

I will conclude by saying that it's as simple as bread.

Bread is a basic staple. Butter with bread makes it more palatable. Butter and jam with bread make it nice and appetizing. Bread, butter and cheese can create a pizza. Bread, butter, jam and cheese is sheer indulgence! In much the same manner, we can keep adding to the most basic aspects to make life more interesting and fulfilling.

TABLE OF MEASURES

LIQUID MEASURES

The cup measure used in this book is 200 ml.

Fluid oz	US	Imperial	Metric
-	1 tsp	1 tsp	5 ml
½	3 tsp/1 tbsp	3 tsp/1 tbsp	15 ml
4	½ cup/¼ pint	-	110 ml
5	-	½ cup/¼ pint	140 ml
8	1 cup/½ pint	-	225 ml
9	-	-	250 ml/¼ litre
10	1¼ cups	1 cup/½ pint	280
16	2 cups, 1 pint	450	
18	2¼ cups	500 ml/½ litre	
20	2½ cups	1 pint	560
32	4 cups/2 pints/1 quart	900	

US/Imperial Measures		Metric Measures	
oz	lbs	Grams	Kg
1		30	
3½		100	
4	¼	115	
8	½	225	
9		250	¼
12	¾	340	
16	1	450	
18		500	½
28	1¾	780	
32	2	900	
36	2¼	1000	1
54		1500	1½
72	4½	2000	2

SOLID MEASURES

Oven Temperature Equivalents

Fahrenheit	Celsius	Gas Mark
225	110	¼
250	130	½
275	140	1
300	150	2
325	170	3
350	180	4
375	190	5
400	200	6
425	220	7

TABLE OF MEASURES

450	230	8
475	240	9
500	250	10